AGAINST *the* TIDE

AGAINST *the* TIDE
Reclaiming Authentic Christian Education

Carl Herbster & Randy Hurst

AMBASSADOR INTERNATIONAL
GREENVILLE, SOUTH CAROLINA & BELFAST, NORTHERN IRELAND

www.ambassador-international.com

AGAINST THE TIDE
Reclaiming Authentic Christian Education
By Carl Herbster & Randy Hurst

© 2011
All rights reserved

Printed in the United States of America

ISBN: 978-1-935507-78-9

Cover Design & Page Layout by David Siglin of A&E Media

AMBASSADOR INTERNATIONAL
Emerald House
427 Wade Hampton Blvd.
Greenville, SC 29609, USA
www.ambassador-international.com

AMBASSADOR BOOKS
The Mount
2 Woodstock Link
Belfast, BT6 8DD, Northern Ireland, UK
www.ambassador-international.com

The colophon is a trademark of Ambassador

Dedication

To the godly pastors, administrators, and faculty who have given their lives to serve the Lord in the ministry of Christian schools, this work is dedicated with gratefulness, respect, and admiration.

Table of Contents

The Philosophy of the Christian School

Why are we in this, anyway?

Every generation is defined by a new struggle. The Christian school movement originated against a tide of opposition from the secular schools and the government establishment. God did many wonderful works, and Christian schools flourished. The current generation must fight against a different tide, one that pulls toward complacency, compromise, and spiritual mediocrity. This downward pull is more insidious, not coming from the outside, but from within. It may come from the distractions and fears that school leaders face, weary of the same old battles. It may come as pressures from the very families whom these leaders serve. To remain faithful to their mission, Christian school leaders must consciously choose to fight against the tide. What would you be willing to do to have the students at your Christian school graduate with a heart for God? What will it take to have Christ-honoring young people going on from your school t' enthusiastically serve the Lord? And is there any limit to what yo are willing to do and to endure to accomplish such a goal?

In the beginning, the establishment of Christian schools w the realm of pioneers: people of vision and courage. Pastors a administrators did jail time in some states because they were "encouraging truancy"—students were attending their schools instead of the public schools. From lack of funds to inexperienced staff, difficulties seemed insurmountable. Pastors, principals, parents, and students cried out to God and saw miracles of provision.

In the beginning, yes, the founders of Christian schools made many mistakes. Their buildings were simple, their programs were limited, and, often, the administrators and teachers alike were as green as June apples. Now, in the maturity of the Christian school movement, many of the schools are full of the best technology but the worst attitudes. The buildings sometimes are better than the graduates. Students may score high academically but low spiritually. It is time to reclaim the passion that drove the founding of the Christian school movement—is there a need to rekindle that passion in your school?

Purpose of Christian Education

Foundations are all–important. Consider how you stand in three areas:

A Biblical Philosophy

The passion for Christian education comes from seeing the orld God's way. Two Greek words, *philo,* love, and *sophos,* wisdom, m the word *philosophy,* "the love of wisdom." In searching for lom, each person develops a system of values and beliefs that his or her actions. This is a philosophy of life.

ne source of your philosophy makes a critical difference. The un must develop his philosophy from God's truth, the Bible: them through thy truth: thy word is truth" (John 17:17). s wisdom that sanctifies, that "sets apart" from the world's , uncertain, self-defeating ways. The Christian philosophy ion is consciously based on Christ, "in whom are hid asures of wisdom and knowledge" (Colossians 2:3). Any leaves one susceptible to worldly influences.

A philosophy of life may be based on true or on false premises. The Apostle Paul warned his readers not be "spoiled"—taken captive as if in a war—by the philosophies of this world (Colossians 2:8). A few people live philosophically consistent lives, but most live with a jumble of different values and beliefs, often unconsciously accumulated. C. S. Lewis observed that modern man is accustomed to having "a dozen incompatible philosophies dancing about together inside his head"—never considering that they are mutually exclusive (Lewis, 1941, p. 11). For instance, a Christian leader cannot believe that God is good and sovereign and yet lose hope that his or her Christian school can glorify God and help family. Belief holds on to God's promises, such as "greater is he that is in you, than he that is in the world" (1 John 4:4). The belief and the emotion are inconsistent, and this discrepancy reveals that some other belief has been interjected into that person's worldview.

Although the Bible does not mention the Christian school, it says much about the education of young people. God makes it plain that His goal for all Christians is that they "be perfect throughly furnished unto all good works" (2 Timothy 3:17). To accomplish this task, God gives people various gifts "for the perfecting the saints, for the work of the ministry, for the edifying of the body of Christ: till we all come in the unity of the faith and of the knowledge of the Son of God, unto a perfect man, unto the measure of the stature of the fullness of Christ" (Ephesians 4:12-13). The goal, then, of Christian education is to create in every young person the likeness of Christ, to develop Christians whose attitudes, actions, and goals in this life anticipate their eventual conformity to the image of Christ (Romans 8:29). Therefore, the purpose of the Christian school is to produce Christlikeness in every young person who attends.

Children must get an education. This common sense observation carries the force of law in modern American society. Compulsory school attendance laws require all educable children within certain ages to attend school, although most jurisdictions make allowances for structured home education. Christian parents, as citizens, are to "be subject unto the higher powers" (Romans 13:1). They obey the law by providing for their children an education within the framework of the required number of years and days per year. The government has provided public schools to help parents fulfill this need.

American public education began with The Old Deluder Satan Act of 1647: "It being one chief project of that old deluder, Satan, to keep men from the knowledge of the Scriptures," schools were established to teach children to read. Parents and civic leaders wanted children to read well enough to understand the Scriptures, and thereby to avoid Satan's deception. The public education system has moved a long way—the wrong way. Now the Bible is legally outlawed and only humanistic values are allowed. The goals of the government school system are only secular. Students are conformed to the mores of society, not to the mind of Christ. The goal is to make them fit into this world system, that is, to be worldly. That goal opposes God's objective. Scripture commands, "Be not conformed to this world, but be ye transformed by the renewing of your mind" (Romans 12:2).

Christian families should not be sending their children out to whatever educational system awaits them. The Christian school exists an alternative to provide education with a biblical framework. Christian schools do not exist to get students away from drugs, gangs, or bad academics. The Christian school has been established to help parents obey God's command to give their children a Christian education. Even if the secular schools could improve in academics or even in their control of drugs, gangs, and violence, the Bible still mandates Christian education. Christian parents need schools where their children receive education presented with a Christian worldview.

It is not what is absent from the Christian school that counts; it is what is present—the influence of Christ Himself. One goal of secular education is socialization, helping the child to fit into society. However, the view of what fits into society is ever changing, and is sometimes opposed to Bible-based values. In John 17 Christ prayed, "They are not of the world, even as I am not of the world. Sanctify them through thy truth: thy word is truth." The goal of the Christian school is not to help children to fit into this world system, but to prepare them to function biblically in this world:

- To function—an education that meets the practical needs of life, teaching varied subject matter from phonics to computer technology.
- Biblically—students learn to evaluate, decide, and act, consciously using God's principles.
- In this world—able to discern error and answer with God's absolute truth in a postmodern culture moving increasingly into secularism and relativism.

Christian schools must teach students not only how to make a living, but also how to live.

A Distinctive Difference

When the Christian school movement began, the distinctives of the Christian schools were accentuated while the similarities were rarely mentioned. Now some Christian schools have begun to emphasize their similarity to the public school as a good thing. They have said that they are the same as the public school, but enjoy the added benefit of a Bible class and chapel. It is a mistake, however, to accentuate the similarities.

The Christian school should be significantly different from the public school. These differences should go well beyond d's code, behavioral expectations, chapel service, Bible class, or life environment. The distinctives of the Christian school ould include Bible-based philosophy and instruction in every subject area. If a Christian school teacher could teach math or English the same way in a public school, that teacher is not distinctively Christian in his or her teaching. Christian schools must not be like the public schools, which, by law, have excluded God. Christian schools must maintain biblical distinctives, or why should they exist?

The focus on a biblical worldview is no excuse, however, for second-best academics. There is no reason for a Christian school to do less than what is required of the local public school in regard to state requirements, even if the state does not mandate that "private schools" have the same graduation requirements. Christian schools should offer academics that equal or excel their states' standards in such areas as the required hours of instruction per year and numbers of credits in math, science, and other areas. Questions of conscience are rarely a challenge in meeting the state's standards. Your Christian school should be known in your community for excellent academics, doing all to the glory of God (1 Corinthians 10:31).

There is also nothing wrong with drawing good teaching techniques from various sources. Christian educators can learn much from the research and experience of other educators, even those from secular schools.

A Focused Mission

Why should parents send their children to your school when they are already paying taxes to support the public school system? You need to define the mission of your school, and you should keep it in front of your people regularly. Rather than continuing that has been because it has always been, keep the purpose of your Christian school warm in your heart and ready in your speech. nts, students, and staff should hear these ideals expressed as a al part of your daily communication, something that flows out of a full heart. If there is a sponsoring church, the pastor should have the same passion, which naturally finds its way to expression in private conversation and in pulpit preaching.

Every Christian school should have a written mission statement. This is one sentence which concisely presents the main goals of the school. Christian school leadership should not simply adopt one from another school; the statement needs to be home grown, reflecting the heart of your local ministry. Because the statement reflects the whole ministry and because the very development of such a statement is a growing process for all involved, the writing of the mission statement is not a one-person job. It is a good project for the administrator and the faculty or a committee chosen *from* the faculty *by* the faculty. They should carefully consider and precisely express what should result from young people being trained in their Christian school. The mission statement is not about process ("having daily Bible class") but about product ("students who know and live God's Word"). Even if Scripture is not quoted in the mission statement, there should be a Bible reason for every idea included.

The following are two examples of mission statements:

XYZ Christian School's purpose is to provide a Bible-based, quality education that inspires each student to pursue excellence in moral character, spiritual growth, and academic achievement; to assist Christian families in training their children to appreciate America's Christian heritage and culture, assume individual responsibility, and be worthy representatives of Jesus Christ; to challenge our students to demonstrate integrity in every aspect of life; and to serve others for the glory of God.[1]

---

1   Based on Upper Bucks Christian School, Sellersville, Pennsylvania.

> The mission and purpose of XYZ Academy is to assist the Christian home in providing a sound education for its children, both academically and spiritually, in a Christ-honoring and caring atmosphere so that each child may be conformed to the image of Christ.[2]

After it is written, the mission statement must be kept in the forefront of everyone's consciousness. It should be stated in as many public and private ways as possible. It should be in handbooks and newsletters and on banners. A mission statement which no one remembers has little value. Choices made by the faculty and administration should reflect the ideals of the school's mission:

- Does a certain choice violate the principles of God's Word?
- Is it consistent with the school's mission statement?
- Does it violate any policy or procedure already in place?
- An effective mission statement is a goal to be actively pursued. It screens options and drives decisions.

The mission statement is a good tool, but it is just a tool. What is needed is not just a well-written statement; it is a group of people who are guided by the biblical principles expressed in that statement. There are many Christian schools floating from year to year without clear direction. Academic and spiritual excellence may be lost by degrees when people lose sight of their mission.

Responsibility for Christian Education

Christian education must proceed from the home. If the parents are not teaching biblical principles at home, chances for success elsewhere are greatly diminished. The Old Testament commands parents, "Teach [God's Word] diligently unto thy children" (Deuteronomy 6:7). The New Testament reflects the same: "Bring them up in the nurture and admonition of the Lord" (Ephesians 6:4).

---

2   Based on Providence Christian School, Riverview, Florida.

These commands are directed to Christian parents, who bear ultimate responsibility for the success or failure of their children's education. Some of the task of educating may be delegated: a child "is under tutors and governors until the time appointed of the father" (Galatians 4:2). Although parents can delegate authority to others as helpers, parents always retain responsibility.

Children must develop a taste for spiritual things in the home. 1 Peter 2:2-3 uses the word *taste* in just this application: "As newborn babes, desire the sincere milk of the word, that ye may grow thereby: If so be ye have *tasted* that the Lord is gracious." To *taste* is "to experience a flavor by taking a small portion into the mouth." To taste something requires experience. Before children can develop an appetite for Christlikeness, they must experience, or take small "tastes," of it in their lives, usually at home first. Upon accepting Christ as personal Savior, they begin to grow as they submit their wills to the will of the Holy Spirit, as they are immersed in God's Word, and as they observe godly people. It is the responsibility of parents, depending on the power of the Holy Spirit, to draw their children to love God, God's Word, and God's ways. As loving parents nurture their children to have a wholesome spiritual appetite, the church and school will have a good base on which to reinforce the biblical training that is taking place at home.

Another institution with God-given responsibilities for education is the church. In the Great Commission Jesus told His church—all Christians—to go and disciple "all nations, baptizing them in the name of the Father, and of the son, and of the Holy Ghost: teaching them to observe all things whatsoever I have commanded you" (Matthew 28:19-20). The church is to make disciples. Disciple-making assumes evangelism; a person must be won to Christ before he or she can be discipled. After evangelism must come education, "teaching them to observe all things."

The Christian school has been established as an extension of the home and, usually, of the church. It has accepted responsibility for reinforcing the biblical teachings of the home and the church. It operates *in loco parentis,* in the place of the parents for certain hours, with authority delegated to it by the home and the church.

Although the teaching of English, history, science, and math are not the direct job of the local church, the church does have an interest in the discipling of the whole person. Intellectual schizophrenia results from trying to believe a "Sunday" worldview and the "Monday" worldview of the secular school at the same time. There are many good, even godly, teachers in the public school system. The only problem is that many legal restrictions limit their freedom to defend God's absolute truth at school. As a result, the core humanist doctrines go unchallenged: evolution, abortion, and the subtle—or sometimes blatant—attacks on everything Christian. These attacks have moved beyond arguments promoting erroneous views. Now a subtler, pervasive assumption of the irrelevance of Christianity sets the tone in secular society. Even the old arguments, such as the secular argument *against* the role of Christian values in the founding of America, had something good: the need to argue suggested that there were some people who believed that Christians *did* play a vital role. More powerful is the smug modern assumption that the debate about Christianity is past, and that the Bible-believing Christians have lost. Any significant references to the influence of the Bible in literature and history were expurgated over a generation ago. Christian history is lost, strayed, or stolen.

Our children in their formative years do not need to be sent into the camp of the enemy to resist the brainwashing of pervasive secularism. Not every church is called to start a Christian school, but every church must be part of equipping and assisting families in this battle for the minds of children and young people. For some, that means establishing a Christian school and doing the serious maintenance required to keep it truly Christian.

One thing that must be understood is that Christian education and the Christian school are not the same thing. Christian education is the *process* of conforming the student to the image of Christ. The Christian school is a *place* designed to give students a part of their Christian education. Even hiring only Christian teachers does not provide a Christian education if they are not succeeding in helping students toward Christlikeness.

Many people assume that once a child is in a Christian school, the child will automatically receive a Christian education. However, many schools that are called "Christian" do not produce students conformed to the image of Christ. A school that is not accomplishing the basic goal of Christian education is not a Christian school. On the other hand, it is possible for a child to obtain a Christian education without ever attending a Christian school. Home education may— or may not—produce Christlikeness. A few students attend secular schools and still come out with a strong Christian worldview, but the fire of humanistic opposition consumes many more young people than it refines. Since attending a Christian school does not guarantee a Christian education, and since a Christian education does not require a Christian school, the two terms are not synonymous and should not be used interchangeably.

The process of Christian education should occur in the Christian school, but the "Christian" label is no guarantee. Perhaps 25% of the students are being conformed to the image of Christ. Perhaps 50%. Even if it were 90%, is that satisfactory? The leadership of the Christian school should never be content until 100% of the school's students are becoming more like Jesus Christ.

Of course, this is an ultimate goal and one which will never be reached here on earth. Even the first Christian school, with

Christian Education and the Christian School

Christian
Education
A Process

Christian
School
A Place

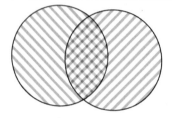

25 % BEING CONFORMED TO CHRIST

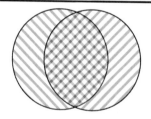

50 % BEING CONFORMED TO CHRIST

THE GOAL:

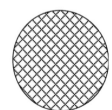

"That we may present every man perfect in Christ Jesus."

Colossians 1:28

100% BEING CONFORMED TO CHRIST

only 12 students and the greatest Teacher of all time, lost one of its students to the world. But the assignment remains to "present every man perfect in Christ Jesus" (Colossians 1:28), and Christian educators must work toward that goal with all the earthly and heavenly powers God provides.

Recipients of Christian Education

Christian education is for Christians. "As education in general begins with physical birth, Christian education properly begins with spiritual rebirth" (Kienel, p. 4). The unsaved person cannot be conformed to the image of Christ because "the natural man receiveth not the things of the Spirit of God: for they are foolishness unto him: neither can he know them, because they are spiritually discerned" (1 Corinthians 2:14). The unregenerate person cannot be expected to conform his life to the Bible because he does not have the Holy Spirit to teach him all truth (John 14:26; 16:13). Without the Teacher there can be no Christian education.

The purpose of the Christian school is not to evangelize the lost, but to educate saved young people to be like Christ. Some schools have established specifically evangelistic admissions policies. They admit any young person who agrees to abide by the standards and rules of the school, whether the young person is saved or lost. This practice forgets that "a little leaven leaveneth the whole lump" (1 Corinthians 5:6). The influence of just a few can cause evil to spread throughout the entire school. Many schools that have operated on an evangelistic philosophy in the past can testify to the problems that have resulted. One student with a powerful personality and a worldly perspective can influence many others the wrong way. The greater the number of students who are not committed to Christlikeness, the greater their influence.

Considering the matter one step further, the Christian school is, generally, for the children of Christian parents. The school must be in agreement with the primary guardians of the students. If the school acts *in loco parentis*, it is philosophically contradictory for the school to be teaching a worldview that contradicts that of the unsaved parents. The school should be reinforcing the biblical principles already being taught in the home. The Christian school and the parents must work together to train young people effectively for the Lord. If there is any conflict between the two, the parents will be frustrated and the mission of the school will be hindered.

One of the challenges facing Christian school administrators today is the tension that sometimes develops between the home and the school. The school and the home must approach the nurturing and character-formation process from the same philosophical position if the school is to be effective in assisting the parents

Are all of the young people in the Christian school saved? No, many of the elementary students may not have come to the point in their lives where they have trusted Christ as Savior. This may be true of some junior high and even senior high students. Sometimes people realize later in life that their profession of salvation was based on an erroneous foundation. For this reason it is very important that clear biblical teaching on salvation be given so that these young people might become "wise unto salvation through faith which is in Christ Jesus" (2 Timothy 3:15). However, the Christian school should not be designed primarily for evangelism. Unless the student body of a school is predominately Christian, the school cannot be considered a Christian school.

The best way to maintain a predominately Christian student body is to have a restrictive admissions policy. Such a policy attempts to admit primarily Christian young people from Christian homes. Parents who want their children to develop Christlike character should be encouraged to enroll their children. Unsaved parents of unsaved young people should not be so encouraged unless they truly desire that their children be saved and conformed to the image of Christ. Many unsaved parents desire only the high academic standards and good discipline that the Christian school offers—and offers with less financial cost than the secular private school which offers those things. Often they do not want the training in godliness that the Christian school exists to provide.

Sometimes a church will have a preschool as an outreach ministry, that is, as a method of evangelism. The goal is to establish relationships with families who need childcare service, whether or not the family has a commitment to Christ. That practice can be good if the preschool is genuinely and actively a soulwinning outreach and not just a money-maker. A clear line must be drawn and understood from the first: the student cannot enter the Christian school unless the parents are willing to go a step further. The dividing line between the preschool and the Christian school might be the beginning of kindergarten or of first grade. The level of commitment required of parents might be their active and regular involvement in your church or a church that you can recommend as being of like faith.

Another special case is the child won to Christ through the evangelistic outreach of the Sunday school or bus ministry. This child or teen could be admitted as long as he or she maintains faithful attendance in a Bible-preaching church. The parents must understand the unique focus of the Christian school and be actively desiring that for their child.

New-family interviews are essential to maintaining the right kind of student population. When enrolling elementary students, the administrator must be especially concerned about each parent's spiritual condition. The administrator must ask about the parents' salvation experience and church background. Many interviews have turned into opportunities to witness. Then the administrator must determine whether or not the parents will support the standards of the school, such as dress, discipline, behavior, and separation issues. If it is clear that the parents will not support the school, the administrator should explain to the parents that they would not be satisfied with the results they would obtain at the Christian school. It should be pointed out that the philosophy of the Christian school would conflict with their teaching at home. When the purpose of Christian education is presented properly, many parents who desire only good academic education will not enroll their children in the Christian school.

The administrator, of course, cannot perfectly discern parents' salvation or values. Even an unregenerate parent can be so agreeable and cooperative that he or she talks like a saved person. The administrator may get to the end of an interview still unsure about these matters. If in doubt, the administrator may decide to enroll the student conditionally or for a trial period. If events later reveal an unsupportive attitude in the parents or a rebellious spirit in the young person, the administrator will have to apply the leaven principle and ask the student to leave.

The interview is especially important in the case of a junior high or senior high student. The parents and the student should be interviewed together. Then the administrator should interview the parents without the teen and the teen without the parents. The focus of the conversation with the parents is their desire for Christian education for their child. Parents must completely support the school if the school is to have a good effect in the life of a secondary student.

The interview with the student focuses first on whether the student wants to do God's will. The administrator must examine the student's understanding of salvation. The interview may become a soulwinning presentation. In fact, many prospective students have responded to the plan of salvation in such an interview. The next purpose of the interview is to determine whether the student will abide by all the rules and requirements of the school. One important question is "Do you really want to attend this school?" If a student entering junior high or senior high does not want to be in that school, problems are likely to arise if he or she is admitted. An unsaved student should be admitted to a Christian secondary school only if the parents are saved and the student shows promise of responding to the claims of Christ. If the student is hardened against the gospel, the administrator must again consider the leaven principle. This discernment takes maturity, experience, and, above all, the leadership of the Holy Spirit. The Christian school cannot be both a reform school for worldly teens and a discipleship school for God-fearing young people.

Some Christian schools use a church attendance policy to help them maintain a primarily Christian student body. This policy requires every student to attend a minimum of two church services per week. Such a policy is a negative in the eyes of most families who want to be in the Christian school for the wrong reasons. If parents are involved in a church that does not have two services per week, they could be pointed to Bible-preaching churches that could provide the other required services. The church attendance policy does not determine which Bible-believing church they attend, just how often. The list of services that count separately toward this requirement may include the following:

- Sunday school
- Sunday morning worship
- Youth meeting
- Sunday evening worship
- Midweek prayer meeting
- Special meetings, such as revival meetings

Since very few people from unsaved or liberal homes will be willing to abide by this policy, the Christian school should be able to maintain a predominately Christian student body.

In these last days before the Lord's return, parents and educators are battling Satan for the lives of young people. This battle can only be won as they train students to be Christlike, equipping them for their own spiritual warfare. The only kind of school that can equip students this way is one that has a biblical philosophy of the purpose for, the providers of, and the recipients of Christian education. A truly Christian school is required. To have that truly Christian school, the leaders of the school must be willing to sacrifice convenience and financial gain. They must accept the pressures of dealing with parents who sometimes misunderstand them and their school. They must patiently and lovingly help families grasp the school's biblical philosophy, as much as the parents will receive (2 Timothy 2:25). They must realize that their school may not appeal to large numbers. And, as leaders they must not only understand that philosophy but must also teach, promote, and defend it in their churches and among their school families.

References:

Kienel, Paul A. (n.d.). *The philosophy of Christian education.* Whittier, CA: Western Association of Christian Schools.

Lewis, C. S. (1941). *The Screwtape letters* (Christian Library ed, 1990). Uhrichsville, OH: Barbour.

Records of the governor and company of the Massachusetts Bay in New England (1853), II: 203. Retrieved 22 June 2006. <http://personal.pitnet.net/primarysources/ deluder.html>

Reclaiming a School for Christ

True to those who depend on you

What type of atmosphere do you have in your school—and who is in control of that atmosphere? What life choices have been made by your graduates of the last three or four years? How many have accepted God's call to the ministry? How many are attending good Christian colleges? If you are not happy with your answers, is God pleased with your school?

Diagnosis

To solve any problem, one must first realize that it exists. Many Christian schools are blind to their own serious weaknesses. Others know they have problems, but lack the resolve to deal with them. Sometimes leaders lack the humility needed to seek help. The lives of Christian young people and the trust that their parents have placed in the school demand honest, bold self-assessment.

The goal of Christian education is always the development of Christlikeness in the lives of the students (Romans 8:29). There are many warning signs when schools are not accomplishing this.

The best way for you to evaluate success in this area is to study the graduates of your school.

Several questions can help assess the spiritual success of your graduates. How many are furthering their education in good Christian colleges? How many of are marrying godly young people who love the Lord rather than marrying unsaved young people? How many are faithfully attending and serving in good, Bible-preaching churches? Are any of your graduates surrendering their lives to full-time Christian work (pastoring, being missionaries, teaching in Christian schools, working at Christian camps)? Not every graduate will be called to full-time Christian work. However, God will call some, and if their teachers and administrators are praying and leading properly, some will respond (Matthew 9:37). Not everyone is called to full-time Christian *work,* but all are called to full-time Christian *service.* All of your graduates should be actively serving the Lord, faithfully participating in Bible-preaching churches, even if they are in full-time secular work. Christian schools should be producing Christlike young people who want to serve the Lord Jesus Christ until He comes again. If a school not experiencing a high degree of success in this mission, it has a problem that needs to be fixed.

You do not need to wait for graduation to evaluate your progress. Ask God to give you the discernment to see what is in front of you every day. If your school has spiritual problems, the students and their parents know all about it. You should too.

Those who visit many Christian schools regularly, such as evangelists or consultants, consistently report a state of dire need. They have preached in Christian school chapels and have seen the carnality and complacency there. Apathy shows on the students' faces: "The show of their countenance doth witness against them" (Isaiah 3:9). Their alienation shows in their dress

(1 Samuel 16:7), and it shows in their activities and in their attitudes toward spiritual things (Matthew 7:20; Matthew 15:18; Romans 8:6, 8; 1 Corinthians 6:19, 20).

You can learn much about the spiritual condition of your Christian school if you spend time with students in the halls, in the lunchroom, and after school. When you talk to young people, the conversation often reveals the spirit of the person (Proverbs 23:7) and the spirit of the place (1 Corinthians 3:1-3).

Athletic events are also prime times for learning about the spirit of a Christian school. It seems that sporting events bring out the best or the worst in people. The players, the cheerleaders, the coaches, and the fans can model Christlikeness or worldliness. Christian school athletic events ought to be different from the over-emphasized and almost-deified athletic activities of the world. Too much emphasis is given to athletics in society, and often that imbalance infiltrates the Christian schools.

The Lord may give you the chance to learn how the high school students live away from school. What kind of friends do they choose outside of school (Proverbs 13:20; 1 Corinthians 15:33)? What kind of music do they listen to when they are alone in the car (Colossians 3:16; Psalm 40:3)? What kind of programs do they watch on TV, on-line, or by DVD (Psalm 101:3; Ephesians 5:10, 11)? Sometimes even Christian school young people smoke, drink, and are immoral (Ephesians 5:3, 4; Colossians 3:5). This should not be!

The truth is that some schools are simply worldly, secular schools with a Christian name. These schools are more dangerous to young people than the public schools. When young people go to a public school, at least they know that it has a secular philosophy of education. However, when they go to a Christian school with a secular philosophy, they are deceived into thinking Christians are no different from the world, a philosophy leading to sure destruction. It is safer for young people to be in a secular school, which they know is secular, than for them to be in a supposedly Christian school that is no different from the world. Your calling is to provide for young people and their families a Christian school which lives out a biblical philosophy of education.

Success is possible. Many Christian schools have been developing Christlike young people for many years. Their graduates are now serving God and raising their own families for the Lord Jesus Christ. Many graduates of Christian schools are now ministering in the Christian school movement, and many have their children attending Christian schools. A Christian school which actively lives out a biblical philosophy of Christian education can consistently produce graduates who love and serve the Lord Jesus Christ.

Prescription

The diagnosis of spiritual problems can be a painful process, but pain is balanced by hope. The Great Physician provides the prescription that will heal wounded schools.

Philosophy—The Foundation

A biblical philosophy of Christian education is the foundation upon which every Christian school should begin. Some schools were started with the wrong philosophy or with no defined philosophy at all. Too many Christian schools were started because of poor discipline in the public schools or poor academics or because the Bible and prayer were expelled from public schools by the United States Supreme Court in the early 1960s. All of these are important issues, but none of them reflect the primary purpose of Christian education.

No matter how they began, many Christian schools are now operating on a secular philosophy with some Bible thrown in.

The average Christian school administrator would have a hard time articulating his or her biblical philosophy of education. The lack of clearly articulated principles leaves a school on slippery ground, and there is a spiritual law of gravity too: things naturally tend to go downhill.

These schools need to be—and can be—reclaimed for the Lord Jesus Christ.

Once the problem is recognized, it is time to communicate a Christian philosophy of education with all of its practical applications. This philosophy is developed from the Word of God, which is alive and powerful (Joshua 1:8; Psalm 119:9-11; John 17:17; 2 Timothy 3:15-17; Hebrews 4:12). Every school stakeholder needs to hear it. It must be preached from the pulpits of churches and in school chapels. It must be taught to parents who want Christlike young people. It must be learned and implemented by Christian school educators. Philosophy is the key, and everyone who is involved in Christian education must understand it, be committed to it, and implement it.

Be honest and forthright in presenting biblical principles to the students. Skip the stealth-philosophy approach. The teaching of God's Word should take place within every class, every chapel, and the informal conversations of staff and students, "for the word of God is quick, and powerful, and sharper than any two-edged sword, piercing even to the dividing asunder of soul and spirit, and of the joints and marrow, and is a discerner of the thoughts and intents of the heart" (Hebrews 4:12). "Wherewithal shall a young man cleanse his way? By taking heed thereto according to thy word" (Psalm 119:9). The preaching of God's Word must be strong and consistent. God's exhortation to leadership is to "preach the word; be instant in season, out of season; reprove, rebuke, exhort with all longsuffering and doctrine. For the time will come when they will not endure sound doctrine; but after their own lusts shall they heap to themselves teachers, having itching ears" (2 Timothy 4:2-3). Young people can take hard preaching, and, in fact, they will thrive on it. Christian educators simply must be courageous in their obedience to God's commands.

People—The School Staff

As a biblical philosophy of Christian education is developed, there must be a commitment among all staff to operate in light of that philosophy. The administrator of the school must be humble enough to learn from exhortation and observant enough to learn from good examples. The administrator must be committed to implementing the biblical philosophy of education throughout the school or must be replaced by someone who is committed to that goal. The administrator then evaluates the teachers to make sure they have the same biblical philosophy manifested in their lives and teaching. You cannot teach what you do not know (Luke 6:40; 2 Timothy 2:2). The school must hire only teachers who are committed to Christian education and who demonstrate Christian living in their own lives.[3] To reclaim a Christian school for the Lord Jesus Christ, there may need to be personnel changes, a process which is never easy.

The faculty and staff must be consistent in the application of biblical truth. People are more affected by example than they are by exhortation. "Your walk talks, and your talk talks; but your walk talks louder than your talk talks." Never should a student or parent be able to accurately accuse the staff of the school of being inconsistent. Leaders must apply God's Word to their own lives and to each decision that is made within the school, just as they exhort the students to do. There is nothing more effective

---

3   Chapter 4 deals with selecting a Christ-honoring faculty and Chapter 5, deals with developing a Christ-honoring faculty.

in biblical character formation than for a student to be able to emulate someone who is walking like Christ!

There are many tools to help school leaders develop biblical philosophy and practice in the staff. Some ministries bring in outside speakers and teachers who can help with this process. Purchasing books on Christian education for staff to read and evaluate is also effective. Going to Christian education conferences where a proper biblical philosophy of education is articulated and demonstrated can be helpful. Taking a trip to a quality Christian school where godly graduates have been developed is extremely valuable. Interacting with the leadership, families, and educators of such a school can provide valuable insights. It is always helpful to see a complex process in action. Such a visit provides an opportunity to learn by observation, and it also gives discouraged teachers convincing evidence that success is possible.

Finally, pray fervently for your staff. Pray often. Pray privately and publically that God will help your staff be effective models and mentors for young people and their families.

People—The Students

The next area that needs to be evaluated is the admission policy. Remember that an unsaved young person cannot receive a Christian education because "the natural man receiveth not the things of the Spirit of God: for they are foolishness unto him: neither can he know them, because they are spiritually discerned" (1 Corinthians 2:14). When a school has too many unsaved young people in attendance, especially in the high school, it is very difficult to provide an environment conducive to Christian education.[4]

It is not recommended that a school eliminate students who are already enrolled, but rather that the school stop enrolling

---

4   The meaning of *Christian education* was discussed in Chapter 1. Enrollment policy options are considered in Chapter 14.

students who should not be there. One way to begin the change is to implement a more restrictive admissions policy in grades seven through twelve. If primarily Christians from Christian homes are enrolled in the seventh grade and above, then there is a growing percentage of the student body in whom the Holy Spirit is working to conform them to the image of Jesus Christ (1 Corinthians 2:13; Philippians 2:13). By implementing a policy such as this over a six-year period, when those seventh graders are seniors, the school will have a different student body and, therefore, a different spiritual tone. Pray that the Lord will work sooner than six years, but in most cases the gradual approach in reclaiming the school is more effective than a more drastic approach. Purging will have to take place when individual student behavior demands it (Proverbs 22:10; 1 Corinthians 5:7). However, dismissing a student simply because he or she has not trusted Christ should be avoided while you are changing your enrollment policy. Deal carefully with the new students coming in, and pray that God will miraculously work on those who are still enrolled (Ephesians 3:20, 21).

Maintain Biblical Standards

In reclaiming the school, it is also important to reclaim the student/parent handbook. The policies it contains and the attitudes it conveys must be consistent with biblical standards. Many times the addition of regulations prohibiting such things as rock music, unchaperoned dating, and inappropriate dress will cause the worldly students not to reenroll. In this way, some of the negative influences in the Christian school may eliminate themselves by withdrawing without the necessity of leadership asking them not to return. The rules demonstrate what the leaders think is necessary to protect young people so that their lives are not damaged or scared permanently. Wisely considered and well presented policies help to communicate what young people ought to "put off" and what they ought to "put on" (Ephesians 4:22-24). Parents who agree with those standards and the importance of them in producing Christlikeness will enroll their children in those schools. Parents who do not agree will go elsewhere. The latter case is regrettable, but it is best for both kinds of family and for the Christian school student body. Remember that two cannot walk together unless they are agreed (Amos 3:3).

If a school is going to produce a Christlike product, the administration must not allow "the works of the flesh" to be in control of the atmosphere through the actions and attitudes of carnal students. Strong standards of dress (Romans 12:1-2; Galatians 5:16-25), behavioral expectations (Romans 12:1), and music (Colossians 3:16) must be maintained. If not, the school leadership is permitting influences antagonistic to the sanctifying work of the Holy Spirit. The Bible clearly states that "the flesh lusteth against the spirit, and the spirit against the flesh: and these are contrary the one to the other: so that ye cannot do the things that ye would" (Galatians 5:17).

The standards and expectations of the school must be high. These policies must be clearly understood and agreed upon by all stakeholders: the parents, the secondary students, the teachers, the administration, and the pastor (if it is a church-related school). Notice that elementary students are not expected to understand and accept all of the policies. It is enough if their parents are committed to them.

Although no two people would independently write all of the rules exactly the same way, there must be basic agreement in maintaining biblical standards if the school and parents are to experience success in developing Christlike character in the students. Everyone must also have a sweet spirit about going along with rules that may not exactly reflect their own choices, understanding the necessity of consistent institutional standards. The Bible is clear in its teachings: there are rights and wrongs in apparel, in the behavior that is expected of believers, and in the music that people listen to and perform. However, schools often must find ways to define clear boundaries as they work with young people. These guidelines may be necessary without being morally right in themselves. Consider, for example, one of the classic problems of dress code, haircuts for young men. A hair style can be wrong: "If a man have long hair, it is a shame unto him" (1 Corinthians 11:14). For the purpose of a school rule, however, the administration has to define what is not "long." The rule may require that hair "be off the eyebrows, ears and collar and be tapered at the sides and back." That is not the only way to define proper hair length, but it provides a fairly clear standard. Hair over the tops of the ears is not morally wrong. However, an attitude that says, "You can't tell me what to do" is morally wrong.

Often, the administration must choose an objectively definable, enforceable standard within a wide band of options. The goal should be to stay as far away from the flesh and the world as possible. If biblical character formation is the priority, serious consideration must be given to standards.

Once the policies and rules have been changed to effectively facilitate Christian education, they must also be consistently and compassionately enforced. Some Christian schools have started with the right philosophy and practice, but through the years have compromised on their consistent enforcement. An unenforced rule in the handbook is counterproductive: it tells everyone that you are not serious about what you say. If you have a rule that does not reflect a priority, say so publically and drop the rule. Do not just ignore policy. Failure to carry through on written policy is a guaranteed way to alienate young people. However, if you retain a rule, carry through. The Lord disciplines those whom He loves, just as a father disciplines his children (Proverbs 3:12; Hebrews 12:6).

Keep the balance: remember to praise those young people who, as part of seeking to please God, are living within the standards of the school. "A word spoken in due season, how good is it!" (Proverbs 15:23, also Proverbs 25:11). Punishment and praise are God's tools for effective enforcement of right behavior. Both need to be utilized effectively.

Christian school leaders must encourage the young people who desire to please God (Rom 14:19; 15:2) and deal appropriately with the scorners (Prov. 14:9; 19:25; 22:10-11). These twin duties require great consistency, patience, love, and wisdom.[5]

Honor and Confrontation

A common problem is that Christian schools honor young people for God-given abilities, such as musical, athletic, or academic skills, without consideration of whether these students honor God. As a result, students who model the wrong kind of character may receive the public honor. The old saying is "Your get what you honor." Christian schools must honor the students who desire to serve and please God, whether or not these students stand out in areas ordinarily associated with "giftedness." Schools should give awards recognizing students with an outstanding servant's spirit or the graduating senior who best exemplifies the ideals of the school. These awards should be very special awards. The spiritual awards should be balanced with the academic, athletic, and fine arts awards, not only in size and price, but also in how they are built up in the eyes of the staff, students, and family.

---

5   Chapters 6, 7, and 8 deal with discipleship and discipline of students.

A spiritual component should be part of all the subjective award and honor structure within the school.[6] Any award requiring deliberation on the part of a faculty member should consider the spiritual component first. Some awards have clearly established, objective criteria, such as the valedictorian award, which is determined solely by the grade point average. In contrast, the class officer nomination process should include the spiritual focus of the young person as the primary component. Young people will respond to the patterns and priorities that the school leaders establish. Authorities must diligently maintain the focus that Christlike character is the main priority in the Christian school. As they do so, a corresponding change in the spiritual atmosphere will take place.

Similarly, being part of special groups, such as sports teams or special music ensembles should require the statement by most of a student's teachers that this person maintains desirable behavior and attitudes. The limitation "most teachers" allows room for human error. One or two teachers may misread a student, but when the majority see a problem, that is a matter requiring caution. Develop objective standards as much as possible to minimize accusations of preferential treatment. For example, define the number of negative teacher references which will prohibit approval for whatever privilege or team membership is being considered. There should also be a seamless connection from philosophy to policy to discipline—and to the paper trail. Having a record of conferences, referrals, and disciplinary actions can save much conflict. Through it all, however, maintain the mindset of discipleship. If a student does not qualify for an office, team, or opportunity, the message must not be "You're not good enough." As much as possible in this difficult circumstance, the

---

6   Sample award descriptions are offered as an appendix.

leader's attitude, words, and actions should communicate, "Let's set some goals and grow in grace."

Do not forget the power of verbal recognition. When the spiritual tone of the school is foremost in the administrator's mind, honoring positive people and actions will be frequent and natural. Mention that you are pleased with how the Bible quiz team did in recent competition. If a parent or administrator from the competing school has a positive word about your athletes' sportsmanship, pass it on to the whole student body in the next chapel.

"Speaking the truth in love" (Ephesians 4:15) is the key to enforcing biblical behavior and developing godly attitudes. If you communicate convictions with compassion, you will produce Christlikeness. However, convictions are too often communicated without compassion and therefore create contention. Christian educators need to speak the truth with kindness and concern, not with condemning or belittling remarks (Ephesians 4:29). However, too many carnal Christian schools are not communicating biblical convictions at all. Leaders may say that they love people too much to confront them about their sin or worldly lifestyles. They may say that the troubling attitudes or actions are not their responsibility. In reality, they may be afraid to confront people. Confrontation is never easy, but it is a requirement of leadership. Communicating compassion without convictions will lead to compromise. A simple balance is required:

Convictions without compassion bring contention.

Compassion without convictions brings compromise.

But convictions with compassion bring Christlikeness.

God faithfully confronts His children through His written Word and through the conviction of the Holy Spirit (1 Thessalonians 5:21, 22; 1 Corinthians 10:31; Joshua 24:15).

The Bible has many *thou shalt's* and *thou shalt not's*. Leaders need to follow God's example and communicate God's truth with God's compassion so that they can be part of reproducing godly character in Christian school students.

Keep a Steady Hand on the Tiller

There must be a commitment to implementing a biblical philosophy of education no matter what the cost if a Christian school is ever to develop godly young people (Proverbs 22:6). This must be a commitment for the whole journey: the "steady hand on the tiller" assumes storm and requires endurance.

You can expect opposition if you seek to change a carnal Christian school to a Christlike one. The devil always fights God's standard of righteousness (Ephesians 6:12, 1 Peter 5:8). Just as God uses people to accomplish His work, Satan uses people to accomplish his (Luke 22:3). Do not be surprised when students, parents, faculty, and even preachers take you to task as you stand for principles: "Yea, and all that will live godly in Christ Jesus shall suffer persecution" (2 Timothy 3:12). Remember, if you do not grow weary in well-doing, you will reap (Galatians 6:9). Purpose to be "steadfast, unmovable, always abounding in the work of the Lord; forasmuch as you know that your labor is not in vain in the Lord" (1 Corinthians 15:58). If you know that you will meet opposition, then welcome it, because it is an honor to be counted worthy to suffer for the Lord—and as a chance to earn your Ed.D. Granted, that abbreviation usually refers to the doctorate of education earned at a university, but it also represents an even higher degree, a degree of spiritual growth:

E—Expect opposition

D—Depend on God

D—Don't Quit!

Every Christian leader will face opposition; therefore, every Christian leader should have a ready defense against the fiery darts of the wicked. These "Don't Quit" verses should be a regularly reviewed part of every leader's scripture memorization:

> *2 Corinthians 4:1—Therefore seeing we have this ministry, as we have received mercy, we faint not.*
>
> *2 Corinthians 4:16—For which cause we faint not; but though our outward man perish, yet the inward man is renewed day by day.*
>
> *Galatians 6:9—And let us not be weary in well doing: for in due season we shall reap, if we faint not.*
>
> *Luke 18:1—And he spake a parable unto them to this end, that men ought always to pray, and not to faint.*
>
> *Proverbs 24:10—If thou faint in the day of adversity, thy strength is small.*
>
> *1 Corinthians 15:58—Therefore, my beloved brethren, be ye steadfast, unmovable, always abounding in the work of the Lord, forasmuch as ye know that your labour is not in vain in the Lord.*

Even though some may resist change, remember that there are parents who desperately want the kind of school which you are trying to provide. They and their children are depending on you: don't quit.

Pray and preach

If you must reclaim your school for Christ, prayer and preaching are essential to the process. Remember, "the effectual fervent prayer of a righteous man availeth much" (James 5:16). As prayer seeks the power of God, preaching brings people in contact with the Gospel, which is the power of God: "For after that in the wisdom of God the world by wisdom knew not God, it pleased

God by the foolishness of preaching to save them that believe" (1 Corinthians 1:21). God has ordained prayer and preaching to accomplish His work. Therefore, as changes are made in the Christian school, you must pray much, and the preaching must be done with power. Preach the biblical truth of Christian education and pray that people will accept it and implement it. Preach the importance of holiness in Christian living and pray that people will discern right from wrong. Preach God's plan that parents raise their children for God's glory and pray that parents will make it their priority. Preach the Gospel that saves people from sin and pray that the Holy Spirit will bring conviction and salvation. Preach the truth of God's Word to a carnal world and pray for revival in the land—and in your school. Preach the importance of Christlikeness for every believer and pray that God's Holy Spirit will conform His children to the likeness of His son.

It is easier to start a school right than to reclaim a school when it was started wrong or has drifted. However, change is possible through the power of God and through the principles of God's Word. Do not be satisfied with a carnal Christian school. Let God give you a Christlike Christian school that is producing graduates who mirror the image of Jesus Christ and who are changing the world for Him. Other schools have changed for the better and so can yours. Remember nothing is impossible when you put your trust in God (Matthew 19:26; Luke 1:37).

The Pastor and the School Administrator

Effective teamwork

The Problems: Extremes Cause Disaster

The most important and the most often neglected relationship in the Christian school is the one between the pastor and the school administrator. To maximize the power of a Christian school to help develop Christlike students, this relationship must be at its very best.

Two extremes are equally bad. In one school the pastor cannot relinquish any significant control to the administrator. All questions must flow through him for a final decision. Every dime spent has his thumbprint on it. Staff members are not invested with significant decision-making authority in their own departments. If the P.E. teacher wants to order new uniforms, the color had better be OK'd by The Boss. But this control comes with a cost. In this type of ministry, the pastor often neglects much-needed time in study, counseling, prayer, and church ministerial functions. The ever-present clamor of day-to-day school management takes over his life and limits his ministry. Meanwhile, if he ever did have a capable school administrator—or a novice with the potential for development—that person would not stay long under such conditions.

The opposite is also a formula for failure. In this ministry the pastor is nonexistent in school affairs. He simply hires a staff to do a job and divorces himself from any involvement in the affairs of the school. If he thinks of the spiritual condition of the students, the welfare of the faculty, or the enrollment and budget, he thinks of them only to pass them off as the administrator's job. This pastor either does not understand the value of the Christian school to the overall church ministry or does not prioritize his schedule to provide the necessary leadership.

Meanwhile, in this second case, the administrator tries to make his own way. At best, he is guessing what will facilitate the work of the whole church-and-school ministry. At worst, this administrator, left on his own, builds his own little empire. This relationship is likely to end in conflict when the pastor and the administrator eventually find themselves at odds over the handling of some critical issue.

The discussion so far has made two important assumptions. It first assumes a school which is related to a local church. The extremes are essentially the same if there is a school board or committee. Board members can be over-controlling or laissez-faire, just as pastors can. There are just more people trying to directly run the school, and they are less present at the school, and hence less aware of the real needs.

The other assumption is that a pastor has a school administrator with whom to work. In a smaller ministry, the pastor may be the administrator. He may appoint a lead teacher to carry out some of the administrative responsibilities. In this case he must learn to delegate with authority, communication, and accountability. Granted, his teachers are busy people too, and he must not abuse them. However, people thrive when they are needed and given a task that stretches their capacities. Another possibility is to hire an assistant pastor who has skills and background which would enable him to work in both the school and the church. This man would be charged with administration of the school, but since the school alone cannot pay his salary, he would also have some responsibilities in the church.

"All churches with schools give lip service to the idea that the school is an integral part of the church's ministry," writes Dr. Keith Wiebe, then pastor of a local church and later president of the American Association of Christian Schools. "But merely having a school under a church's ministry umbrella does not automatically make it 'integral' " (2002, p. 307). He cites a potentially fatal flaw revealed in the use of language. People do not speak of "the body and the hand" because the hand is part of the body. So, people should not speak of "the church and the school." This phraseology misses the point that the school is just one ministry of the church and promotes an "us versus them" mentality between the different ministries of the local church. Having the school *integrated* into the church ministry requires the right involvement of the pastor and the school administrator.

The People: Extreme Commitment is Good

The Christian school is a major part of a church ministry. Don Forrester holds a doctorate in education, has been a Christian school administrator, and now pastors a church with a Christian school. He presented the following at the National Congress on Christian Education:

> It is true that the school ministry is only one ministry
> of an active church. However, the nature of the school,

in that it consumes such a large portion of the time, energy, and financial and human resources of the church, requires that it receive the special attention and care of the pastor. The administrator should have a visible position of ministry in the congregation to help him establish a testimony of spirituality and a heart for ministry …. Just as the pastor needs a working knowledge of the school, the administrator needs a healthy respect for the ministry as a whole (2002, pp. 324-325).

Unity of Vision

Before entering into a relationship, the pastor and administrator must agree on two things. First, they must be unified on their *philosophy* of education. The primary issue is the purpose of the Christian school. They should be in agreement on these basics: (1) The atmosphere among the student body should be set by young people who desire to please God, who understand that they should work hard in every aspect of school life, and who have a desire to be used by God now and in future ministry. (2) The graduate should be a mature, well-educated young adult with a heart for God, faithfully serving Him, and actively making a difference for the cause of Christ. This "agreement" is more than just a nod to glittering generalities: it must be the passionate drive that directs the labors of each of these leaders.

The pastor and administrator must also be unified on the major elements of the *process* that is necessary to produce that kind of school and that kind of graduate. Everyone in Christian education wants a Christ-honoring atmosphere in the school. They want graduates with a passion to serve God. Some, however, are not willing to implement the process that is necessary to bring those desired outcomes. The process must be biblical, must be deliberate, must be consistently applied, and certainly must be understood by all people in leadership roles in the church and school.

Distinction of Roles

The pastor and school administrator must have a unity of vision and a diversity of function. As team players, they have vital but different roles in the Christian school. On a football team, there are many positions that must be played well if the team is to win. The lineman may want to play quarterback, but, if he leaves his position to rival the quarterback, he is going to get sacked by an opponent coming through the hole he left in the line! On major league teams, even the coaches limit their attention to specific aspects of the game. Every person connected with the team plays a specific role; everyone must perform at 100%.

The home is another parallel. The Bible has provided a job description for each person in a family (Ephesians 5:22-6:4). There is an expectation that every person in the family will play his or her position well while recognizing the vital role others are playing within the family structure.

The pastor and the overall ministry.

The senior pastor establishes the priorities for the whole ministry, including the school. In any ministry, four priorities must be maintained in order:

1. *Philosophy:* Philosophy is first. What is the basic, non-negotiable purpose of the school? This sense of mission proceeds from the work of God in leading the pastor. There may be variations in detail, but one thing is necessary: if the focus becomes anything less than developing Christlike character in students, the school is doomed.

2. *People:* After there is a right philosophy, then people are found to build the ministry within that philosophical paradigm. If

the pastor starts by hiring a really good administrator or teacher who does not share his philosophy, all that he has accomplished is to hire someone who will be really good at taking the school in a direction that God has not called that pastor to go.

3. *Programs:* Good people with the right philosophy are then entrusted to develop programs which will accomplish the goals of the philosophy. For instance, in developing curriculum, the first question is "How will this material or activity develop Christlikeness in young people?" The pass/fail evaluation for the music program, sports, or any other aspect of the school must relate back to the first priority: "Is it accomplishing our philosophical goal?"

4. *Plant:* Buildings and grounds are the last priority. You show your regard for your God by the effort and investment you make in that which bears the name "Christian." The facilities should be the best they can be, within the constraint of wise fiscal management, without being gaudy or ostentatious. They should always be clean and orderly, because you serve an orderly God. However, nice buildings do not make a good Christian school. All is vain without the right philosophy implemented by the right people in effective programs.

The New Testament uses the words *pastor, elder,* and *bishop* to refer to the same office in the church. The *pastor* leads and feeds the flock. The *elder* is the one with spiritual maturity. However, the term *bishop,* the overseer or supervisor, best fits the pastor's role in the school. The pastor is called by God to oversee every ministry of the church, including the school. As such, he cares deeply about the condition and progress of the students and staff, and of the school as a whole.

It is the pastor who keeps the unity of the ministry, including the Christian school as part of the church, in front of the people. At a Congress of Christian School Education, Pastor Peter Foxx presented this:

> Where does the pastor verbalize the philosophy of church and school unity? Obviously, the most effective platform he has for communicating this and other key doctrines is the pulpit. This is exactly why it is so important to have the core of the school staff [in] the local church. ... Like other core truths, if there is no campaign to trumpet the message, it will die a natural death. (2002, p. 313)

The pastor must preach this message—and the full-time staff, at least, should be present, hearing it as members of that local church.

If the pastor has a strong background in school management, he may have many ideas about the daily function and future plans of the school. Yet he needs to work through his administrator. If school management is not the pastor's strength, the administrator will not only inform the pastor of plans and actions, but will also help him to see the reasoning behind them and why certain directions are better than others. In either case, the pastor stays informed and involved. God will lead the school primarily through the pastor.

The pastor and the school.

The senior pastor has distinct tasks in regard to the school. His leadership in the school is emphasized as he meets with the faculty at the beginning of each school year for one or two sessions and, perhaps, at times during the year as needed. After that, the administrator is the primary spokesperson for the philosophy of the ministry and the pastor's direction. A pastor may impede the school administrator's growth and ministry by inserting himself into the role of decision maker too frequently. Instead, he should mentor the administrator, developing in him or her the skills necessary to accomplish the goals of the ministry and to capably express ministry philosophy and policy.

The pastor should work with the administrator in some major decisions. The school is a major part of the overall church budget. There must be collaboration on the development of the school portion of that budget. The tasks each assumes in that collaboration will vary according to the different skills of these people.

He needs to play a pastoral role in the school as a counselor and consoler, especially during times of great trial. As pastor to the whole ministry, he should speak in chapel regularly. This will allow him not only *to set* the spiritual temperature, but also *to measure* it. The pastor can gain valuable insights into the condition of the students by observing how they sing in chapel and by observing their response to his preaching of God's Word. Even on Sunday, he is the pastor of the school, preaching and teaching the importance of Christian education. For the school to continue to succeed, the congregation as a whole must remain committed to its mission.

Suspensions and expulsions, used properly by a wise administrator-pastor team, can be tremendous tools used by God to produce change in the lives of parents and students. But the pastor and administrator should be in communication about these events.

The pastor should be involved in evaluating the spiritual product of the school. Are most of the students going on to Christian colleges? Are those entering secular professions doing so with a heart to serve God in those arenas? Are alumni actively serving in Bible-preaching churches five years after graduation?

Still, the pastor should let the administrator administrate. Hire a good person with the right philosophy, give the authority to get the job done, and let that person do it! But stay in touch. Even though the pastor may delegate the task, he retains the ultimate responsibility. Delegate and give authority, but maintain accountability.

"Pastor, your Christian school needs you." Dr. Jack Scallions, after 35 years of pastoring, leading a Christian school for 25 years of that time, analyzed the need for pastoral involvement in an article by that title. This article is reproduced as an appendix because of its excellent insight into the origins of the Christian school movement, its analysis of current needs, and its practical suggestions. Pastoral involvement is essential to the success of the Christian school.

The administrator implements the philosophy.

The administrator must recognize the responsibility to develop quality programs in academics, fine arts, and athletics. Administrative leadership includes the responsibility of enforcing the regulations which are necessary to maintain a Christlike atmosphere. Sometimes the school administrator is part of the pastoral staff of the church. Forrester endorses this approach: "The role of administrator is a pastoral function. He often oversees the largest portion of the church's budget and the majority of the church's employees" (2002, p. 324). As a result, the school administrator has great responsibility and has great opportunity for spiritual influence. The administrator should be Christlike in demeanor and methods and should provide biblical counsel; but the administrator should not rival the senior pastor for the leadership of the people.

The administrator leads the school ministry. The pastor will lead the whole ministry, but the pastor must establish an atmosphere in which the administrator is recognized as fully in charge of the school. The administrator should not be viewed as simply a puppet of the pastor, but as a key staff member. The administrator should be recognized as a mature Christian, called to an important ministry position and capable of handling its many burdens. The pastor must also ensure that the administrator has the time and the freedom to lead effectively.

If the pastor has been led by the Lord in the hiring process, the administrator is not only the person whom the pastor has hired to run the school, but also the person whom God has called to that task. As the pastor and administrator meet, the pastor communicates his vision to the administrator. The administrator then communicates that vision to the whole constituency of the school: faculty, staff, students, and parents. The administrator must develop healthy relationships with both the pastor and the faculty in order to effectively lead the school.

Synergy in Teamwork

The administrator and the pastor should each value and appreciate the role which the other person plays.

In the pastor-administrator team are two mature, effective leaders. Each is called and empowered by God. Each working alone can get good things done. However, working together, with the blessing of God, they can get *great* things done. Their teamwork, functioning as coordinated members of the Body of Christ (1 Corinthians 12), makes their combined work greater than the sum of their individual works. This is synergy.

The mutual respect between pastor and administrator must be apparent to all. The pastor of a local church must always be treated with the utmost respect and consideration. He is the person called by God to lead the entire ministry and to provide oversight. It is, therefore, critical that the person he hires to lead the school be philosophically aligned with him and able to support him in his role of oversight. Correspondingly, the pastor is helping himself when he lets everyone know that he respects and trusts the administrator.

Communication is essential. An effective school administrator can be a tremendous blessing to a pastor and to the local church. However, if the school administrator is determined to go his own way, he can do tremendous damage.

It is best for the pastor and administrator to meet weekly. These weekly meetings will provide many things:

- The pastor keeps his finger on the pulse of the school ministry.
- The pastor mentors the school administrator.
- The administrator gets counsel and support from the pastor
- Mutually, they
  - Synchronize their understanding of needs, problems, and opportunities,
  - Provide mutual accountability in their different tasks,
  - And brainstorm regarding the ongoing programs and the future of the school.

The meeting agenda should focus on significant disciplinary issues, employee concerns, and anything else that the pastor needs to know. It does not need to include the routine details that can be handled by an able administrative team. The main things should stay the main things. Even in the best of relationships, there will be differences of opinion and different ways to deal with needs. A wise pastor will allow full discussion of any matter and will listen with an open mind. Often a pastor who has some reservations will still yield to the administrator's ideas, realizing the administrator's special expertise in school matters.

This can also be a time of bearing one another's burdens in prayer and counsel. The mentoring and communication aspects of this regular meeting are vital to keeping the spiritual fires burning hot within the Christian school. As one of the pastor's primary fellow-laborers, the school administrator may become a close friend, advisor, and prayer partner with him; and certainly the pastor will be that for the administrator.

If the pastor works with a female administrator, he needs to be cautious. People develop deeper relationships with others with whom they spend much time, especially when they are dealing with something to which they share a deep, mutual commitment, like Christian education. Also, an emotional bond naturally develops through counseling and consoling. Therefore, the basic precautions that any pastor should take in counseling a woman should be in place in any extended meeting with a female school administrator, including the regular weekly meetings. Never meet in seclusion. There should be no late meetings when no one else is in the building. Keep your door open with someone such as a secretary not far away, or meet with the door open to a hallway with people passing. For appearances sake and for the reality of temptation, the pastor and a female administrator need to be wise.

Three levels of consultation develop over time. Some things the administrator just does with no reporting. These are normal matters within the realm of his or her authority. Some things the administrator does, knowing what the pastor would want done, and informs the pastor afterward. On some things, however, the administrator should check with the pastor before taking action. The understanding of what actions fall into which category is unique to each ministry and grows with time.

Job descriptions help everyone function in harmony. Included in the appendix are suggested job descriptions for the school administrator and for the pastor regarding his role in the school. Of course, these are just suggested starting points, and the descriptions will grow and change as any given pastor-administrator team develop their relationship.

The pastor and administrator cooperatively communicate their vision for the school. All school personnel must have a thorough understanding of the goal in order to achieve maximum effectiveness. For example, if the pastor and administrator have a goal of producing "Champions for Christ," both should communicate that consistently. But what is a "Champion for Christ"? Further definition and description is vital. The wise leadership team will consistently express the goal in terms of observable outcomes. The team will also continue to evaluate how each part of the ministry helps to achieve those outcomes. For example, do the pastor and administrator desire to have the vast majority of the Christian school graduates choosing to attend good, fundamental, Christian colleges? If this is a goal, then they should be sure that the parents, students, and faculty are regularly instructed and challenged about the importance of Christian higher education.

The wise pastor and administrator will consistently cast a vision for the ministry and will empower the faculty and staff with freedom to come up with creative ideas to accomplish that vision. While staff members do not have freedom to establish policy, every staff member must be given the freedom to make decisions within the framework of established policy. People take ownership of what they control, and those are the things which they believe in most fervently and work at most diligently. By ensuring that the entire staff is functioning as a godly example for the students, the leadership team will multiply their efforts. Then it is not just the pastor and administrator leading. All the staff are functioning as loving disciplers of the young people, helping them grow in Christlikeness.

With unity in their purpose, understanding of their distinct roles, and teamwork founded upon mutual respect and facilitated by communication, the pastor and school administrator become a powerful team in the work of God.

The Practices: Extreme Consistency Is Necessary

Supporting One Another

Leadership can be very lonely! Every pastor or school administrator who has consistently made the tough decisions understands that. However, God did not design Christian workers to be Lone Rangers. One of the great privileges of ministry is the fellowship of adversity—strong friendships are forged in the fires of affliction. God intends that co-laborers encourage one another: "exhorting one another, and so much the more as you see the day approaching" (Hebrews 10:25). Aaron and Hur held up Moses' hands, and Israel prevailed in the battle as they did so (Exodus 17). There is joy in ministry as the pastor and administrator support and exhort each another.

Exhortation involves more than emotional encouragement, although that is part and everyone needs that sometimes. It also involves direction. Notice how Proverbs 27:9 combines the emotional and the intellectual aspects of exhortation: "Ointment and perfume rejoice the heart: so doth the sweetness of a man's friend by hearty counsel." The word *rejoice* refers to the emotional aspect, and *counsel* refers to the intellectual.

In private discussion, the pastor and the administrator should discuss school matters openly and honestly. "The relationship should foster problem solving. The pastor and administrator must not view each other as antagonists, rather as comrades in arms" (Forrester, 2002, p. 325). This relationship requires that each be secure in the strength and sovereignty of God and in his or her own calling from God to this particular work. Without that security, discussion is hindered by fear of what the other person will think or do. Knowing that God is the ultimate authority, they can privately, lovingly, yet as strongly as necessary, state perspectives that will assist in charting the best possible course for the ministry. Each must be lovingly confrontational in any matter, probing until a mutual understanding has been reached. They must also be secure in their relationship with each other. Trusting each other enough to be transparent about their thoughts and feelings, they develop an "iron sharpeneth iron" relationship (Proverbs 27:17).

It takes time for two people to synchronize their perspectives. Their time spent in weekly meetings provides this benefit. If the school administrator is a man, he and the pastor would also benefit from extended time together, as on trips to educators' conferences or teacher recruitment trips at Christian colleges. They can use these longer periods of time to analyze the present and to seek God's leading for the future (Forrester, 2002). If the administrator is a woman, perhaps the pastor and his wife, with the administrator (and her husband, if she is married) can take that trip together. A deeper understanding of all involved and a more powerful teamwork will result.

While the pastor and administrator must feel the freedom for honest disagreement and discussion about various aspects of the school, they must be absolutely supportive of one another in public and in all private conversations with others. Sometimes, even after all the discussion, complete agreement may not be reached. At that point, the administrator must yield to the pastor as the biblical authority within the church (Hebrews 13:7). This stage will not often be reached. A wise pastor will not lightly ignore the advice of one of his primary counselors in regard to the school. A wise pastor also will give the administrator a degree of freedom in decision making. If he does not, he might as well not hire an administrator. However, by the time their conference is over, there is no "my view" or "his view," just "our decision." Even if private differences persist, they must present a public unity. They are not dishonest by denying any differences; they just choose to focus on the final course of action and the reasons behind it. The pastor and administrator should try to avoid airing their differences before others.

This balanced approach allows the pastor and administrator to model the handling of staff relationships. Of course, along with the example should come instruction and accountability. If all staff members handle interpersonal relationships in this biblical manner, much more can be accomplished for the cause of Christ.

Sometimes strong leadership can produce an atmosphere where the staff is afraid to provide counsel that is vital to the decision-making process. This should not be so. One sign of a healthy ministry is that all staff members know that they are *valuable to* the ministry—they have something to give—and that they are *valued by* the ministry—their superiors are willing to genuinely listen to them.

Discipline

School discipline matters are the responsibility of the administrator, but they require measured involvement and complete support from the pastor.

The pastor's measured involvement reflects the levels of discipline. Discipline for minor offences is always best handled at the level closest to the students involved. Much of this is done by the teachers without direct involvement from the administrator or the pastor. The administration should provide for teachers a consistent and well-conceived disciplinary program, easily utilized by each teacher, easily understood by students and parents, and easily managed by all school personnel.

When students commit more serious offenses or if a student is causing on-going problems, the administrator may need to be involved in attempting to disciple or salvage a child and, perhaps, the family. The administrator might begin consulting with the pastor at this stage.

Whenever there is consideration of suspension or expulsion, the pastor certainly must be informed of the details and should lend his counsel and support. Some pastors desire to be a part of these decisions before they are made, some just desire to be informed after the fact, and some, tragically, do not care to know. There should be the kind of private conference between pastor and administrator that allows all frank discussion and consideration. After that, the administrator should be the one seen as the disciplinarian so that the pastor may be seen primarily as one who counsels and restores. Yet, if pressed, the pastor must completely support the decision. It is still "our decision."

If a pastor desires to have a school with a Christlike atmosphere producing graduates with a passion for God, he must be involved in the school. He not only provides counsel to the administrator, but also support in answering those who criticize the administrator. Any time a difficult decision is made by the administrator, some people will misunderstand or disagree. A house divided against itself cannot stand (Matthew 12:25), and neither can a church-school ministry. The support of the pastor is imperative. The pastor must understand:

- The need to produce godly students.
- The biblical process that is necessary to achieve that goal.
- The need for courage to support the tough calls that are made.
- The need to persuade the congregation that biblical standards are necessary.
- The need to teach the congregation what true compassion, love, grace, and mercy are.

The administrator must have the mindset of a discipler, and this must be obvious to all. But he must also be vitally interested in another key component of true discipleship: loving and firm accountability. Students, and even teachers, make choices that demand consequences. The wise administrator will recognize the significant role that loving accountability will play in the lives of students and faculty, and the wise pastor will provide complete support and measured involvement.

The pastor and school administrator complement each other's roles. They must agree in philosophy, policy, and practice. Time spent praying and bearing one another's burdens helps to create an atmosphere where two strong leaders can enhance each other's ministries.

The adversary is a master deceiver who especially desires to destroy the leadership. He knows the devastating effect upon the lives of the faculty, parents, and students when he can tear down a leader. He knows how to sow discord among the brethren and how to attack a work of God. He will not simply surrender because godly people have won, by God's grace, a few battles.

In spite of all this, God can use the ministry of the Christian school to assist parents in the spiritual development of the next generation of leadership in the church. The Lord uses Spirit-filled people to accomplish this task. The Lord desires that each person within a Christian school staff do his or her own part effectively, with enthusiasm and skill, guarding against the weakness of the flesh.

Both the pastor and administrator have vital roles to play in developing and maintaining a Christ-honoring Christian school.

References

Forrester, D. (2002). The relationship between the pastor and the principal. *Congress 2002 on Christian education.* East Ridge, TN: American Association of Christian Schools.

Foxx, P. (2002). Keeping the church and school aspects of ministry philosophically united. *Congress 2002 on Christian education.* East Ridge, TN: American Association of Christian Schools.

Scallions, J. (2001). Pastor, your Christian school needs you. *Journal for Christian Educators,* 8 (1), 10-12.

Wiebe, K. The school as an integral part of the church's ministry. *Congress 2002 on Christian education.* East Ridge, TN: American Association of Christian Schools.

Selecting a Christ-honoring Faculty

People are the key

Philosophy is first. After that the most important ingredient in a successful Christian school is competent, Christ-honoring people. A Christian school will only be as good as the faculty that serves there. One or two great teachers can be pace setters: models to the staff and encouragers to parents and students. One or two weak teachers—academically or spiritually—can ruin the reputation of a Christian school and limit its ministry. But to have "team depth," that is, to have a group of teachers who share a high level of expertise and a deep commitment to the mission of Christian education, is a goal to strive for. It is a *goal* and not a *dream* because it can happen, because it can happen only through prayerful planning and diligent work, and because it will not happen by chance.

Team depth goes beyond the teaching staff. Every staff member must be a born-again Christian whose life evidences the fruit of the Spirit (Gal. 5:22-23) and testifies to the students of the grace of God. The godly janitor can be a powerful influence in the lives of students, but the critical, negative lunchroom worker can erode the work of all the staff. Every staff member counts. Each one must possess a servant's heart, a discipler's approach to every situation, and a desire to be used of God.

Because teachers wield such influence, their spiritual and academic qualifications are vital. A Christian school will never be any better than its people. The teaching staff must be prepared academically as well, since the faculty determines the quality of the education offered: "The disciple is not above his master: but every one that is perfect shall be as his master" (Luke 6:40).

Each teacher must be qualified by training, knowledgeable in academic content, and competent in pedagogy. However, spiritual direction is the most important thing. "It is easier to train a teacher to be more effective in the classroom than it is to help him cultivate a servant's heart" (Deuink and Herbster, 1984, p. 86).

The faculty and staff must be dedicated to one task: allowing God to use them to produce biblical character in the lives of each young person through every academic area and every extracurricular program. Their natural approach is to use every interaction and activity toward one goal: "that we may present every man perfect in Christ Jesus" (Colossians 1:28). The goal of academic excellence must not be an end in and of itself. It is an important goal, but it is accomplished as part of the most important goal, developing Christlikeness in young people.

The hiring process must be thorough and careful. These are the most important decisions that school leaders will make. A Christian school faculty who desire to please God will help students develop Christlike character.

Determine the Needs

The process of assessing next year's staff needs should begin by the middle of October. A good administrator is in touch with the faculty. Through the process of formal conference and evaluation, in casual observation, and by friendly interaction, the administrator can usually tell if a teacher may be considering other options for the future or, perhaps, needs to make a change. God often moves His soldiers strategically on the battlefield. The administrator should not be distressed if God's hand is on one of his teachers. God has a plan for the school which the teacher is leaving as well as for the place to which the teacher is going. If a teacher is struggling with adequately fulfilling responsibilities, the administrator should begin early to help. One of the most fulfilling roles of the administrator is faculty development, a kind of discipleship. But even as this training and encouragement goes on, the administrator must be working on a back-up plan in case a replacement is necessary.

Contracts or statements of intent[7] for the next school year should be given to the teachers by the week before Christmas break. This timing allows the teacher to spend some of the Christmas break deliberating, if necessary, about whether to return.

A deadline of mid-January should be set for the return of signed contracts or statements of intent. This allows the administrator time to converse with a few who may be struggling with the decision. By February, when the teacher recruitment conference season comes, the administrator should understand well the needs of the year ahead and should be able to intelligently recruit needed faculty.

Look in the Right Places

A Christian college is a wise place to look for teachers just beginning their careers. In secular colleges the assumptions about the nature of man and the history, purposes, and processes of education are often deeply flawed. Even if the philosophy is not

---

7   The letter of intent is a form asking the teacher to indicate whether he or she is returning, not returning, or undecided.

anti-Christian, many important areas are ignored. Some Christians come out of secular colleges as excellent Christian educators, but the secular school background presents a set of caution areas for the administrator to consider.

There are other reasons for caution about looking for teachers from secular sources:

> It is almost as important to avoid provoking an interest in those who would not qualify for the position as it is to locate those who will meet the qualifications. Unintentionally soliciting unqualified people creates two problems. First, if an interviewer is not sufficiently thorough, or if an applicant does not answer questions honestly, it is possible to fail to discover things in the applicant's background that would disqualify him spiritually. Administrators occasionally become careless, assuming that those applying for a position in a Christian school already understand and agree with the spiritual standards. Second, a person judged to be unqualified because of spiritual standards may become belligerent and attempt to take legal action against the school on the basis of discrimination. While the chances of his success in such an action are rather remote at this time, the legal expense and public attention created would not be helpful to the school's ministry. (Deuink and Herbster, 1984, p. 92)

Granted, a Christian college background does not guarantee a perfect fit, but it is a good place to begin.

Many Christian colleges provide career placement services used by students nearing graduation and even by alumni who graduated years before. Christian school organizations also offer teacher placement services on line and in print. Schools make their needs known there, and teachers seeking positions post their names and teaching fields.

Whatever source the administrator goes to, it should be an organization that reflects the philosophy of the hiring school.

Veteran or New Teacher?

Hiring a teacher who has years of positive experience is an attractive option. However, the number of years in teaching does not tell the whole story. Caution is appropriate even when—or especially when—hiring veteran teachers. It is important to realize that the fact of having taught for several years does not necessarily mean that the teacher has improved during those years. The teacher may have made the same mistakes throughout his or her entire career, thus providing a less attractive option than a first-year teacher who can be discipled and developed more easily. On most occasions, the older the faculty applicant is, the more firmly he or she is established in philosophy and methods. Experience can be good or bad. A teacher may be firmly established or may be stuck in a rut. Experience is good, but it is critical that the administrator research that experience carefully. Has the experience been positive? Is the teacher growing? Is the teacher teachable? How readily does the teacher leave a school? If a teacher has moved from school to school with short stays, the hiring administrator needs to know why, and he needs to hear the viewpoints of former employers as well as the viewpoint of the prospective teacher. The administrator must also find out whether the veteran teacher's philosophy and practice are in harmony with those of the ministry which the administrator represents.

The other option is the recent college graduate. Granted, it is an exaggeration to say that the four-year education degree merely gives one the right to learn how to teach during the first year in the classroom. Colleges are increasingly requiring that their education majors obtain earlier and more extensive experience in the role of the teacher. The new teacher is not entirely a novice. However, the young adult who begins his or her career in your school will more readily adopt your philosophy and practice as part of the natural growth in teaching. The administrator of that new teacher's first school has a great opportunity for discipleship. There are, however, three requirements for success in this endeavor. First, the new teacher must start within the parameters of the school's philosophy of education. It is probable that a new teacher's philosophy will be deepened by experience and focused by application. It is less probable that the teacher's erroneous ideas on major principles will be corrected. Second, the new teacher must respect the concept of chain of command. Third, the administrator must be observant of the new teacher's needs and be prepared to provide mentoring.

So which is the better option? There really is no better option, and God certainly provides for His people and His schools both ways. The administrator simply must be aware that there are distinctive sets of opportunities and cautions involved with hiring either the veteran or the new teacher.

Three Stages of Recruitment

The process of selecting a Christ-honoring faculty may be analyzed in three distinct phases.

Stage One: Getting to Know Each Other

The administrator should be building relationships with prospective teachers even before he or she knows the needs of the upcoming year. The administrator can maintain contact with education majors—especially graduates of his or her own high school—through the college years. If the administrator has kept an active and accurate account of underclassmen at various colleges, these early contacts with the students will help in the recruitment process.

Many Christian colleges host teacher recruitment conferences at which administrators will be able to make contact with a number of potential teachers. Most colleges will allow, even facilitate, contact with their education majors even before the recruitment conferences. The wise school administrator will make contacts early and often with potential teachers. The administrator certainly would prefer to make a decision between seven or eight qualified candidates rather than to approach the last days before the new school year still trying to fill teaching positions.

Obtaining good results from the teacher placement conferences requires diligent preparation. The effort is worthwhile because the faculty will make or break the school. Therefore, appropriate planning and care must be given to this aspect of administration.

A letter

A letter could be sent in advance of each recruitment conference to the students with the appropriate training. The letter presents the particular need for their teaching fields and encourages them to stop by the school's display at the conference to discuss the possibility of a position. A follow-up telephone call by a secretary to set up an interview is also helpful.

A well prepared display

A well prepared display communicates your message. This message is both the overt—words and pictures tell what your school is like—and the subtle—craftsmanship and choice of materials imply a message about the quality of the school. Therefore, this display should be of high quality. This is one area worthy of significant financial investment. Quality usually comes with a cost. To help justify the expense, this display could be utilized in a number of ways:

- Monthly open houses for prospective parents
- Christian School Day in the local church
- Accompanying a ministry team to area churches

- Summer camps, baseball leagues, games, or awards nights
- Events which bring nonschool families to church activities, such as men's retreats, ladies' retreats, or couple's events.
- School functions that brings nonschool parents to school activities, such as friends and families coming to programs and graduations
- During reenrollment time to remind school parents and to attract others who are not yet enrolled.

Quality informative material

Quality informative material that will positively present the school should be available at the display table. The following are possibilities:

Selected Pictures of the Students and Staff

These pictures may be shown on the background of the display or in another fashion, such as a PowerPoint slide show. It is always good public relations to highlight any current faculty members that have come from the college you are visiting or recent high school graduates who are currently students at that college.

A Prospective Teacher Packet

The packet should be of high quality and should present your school accurately and positively to prospective teachers. It should include the most important elements of your mission. It should also include the differential advantages of your school, those things which make your school stand out from all the rest. The packet could also include a school brochure containing a fuller statement of the educational philosophy of the ministry and the mission statement of the school. In addition, the benefit package, salary scale, faculty requirements, and faculty application, should be included in the packet. Much time and effort should be invested in organizing a large amount of pertinent information into a high quality presentation for the prospective teacher.

Two Most Recent School Yearbooks

These would be for viewing at the booth and not for open distribution. Yearbooks are too expensive to give away.

School Calendars

If the school prints a quality school calendar for the parents, it may be worthwhile to print extra copies for the purpose of teacher recruitment. This would provide valuable evidence of a busy and exciting campus with much to offer a new teacher.

School Newsletters

A newsletter demonstrates the type of communication that takes place between school and parents and how that communication reinforces the philosophy of the school. A newsletter designed to engage and encourage parents will engage and encourage potential teachers too.

School Handbooks

The handbook provides important information for the serious inquirer. Since these books are expensive to produce, they should be available upon request, but they are not set out for every casual passer-by to pick up.

School Paraphernalia

Items with the school name, address, and logo should be freely distributed to prospective teachers. Pass out pencils, pens, key chains, etc., with the name of the school on them. Quality is the name of the game when you are attempting to capture the prospective teacher's attention.

A Sign-up Sheet

The sign-up sheet is a practical step to inform you of a prospective teacher's interest. It should have places for the following: major, minor, year graduating, teaching field interests, and immediate plans. *Immediate plans* are factors that might affect when the teacher would be available, such as graduate school, short-term secular job to pay off a college bill, or marriage. In the case of an upcoming marriage, both members of the engaged couple should be in favor of the teacher's going to your school. Take the initiative and be enthusiastic when speaking with prospective teachers. Do not be afraid to speak about the distinctives and the strong points of your school. Most prospective teachers are looking for strong leadership, a quality school program, a school producing a quality graduate, and a commitment to excellence.

It is also important to be truthful and accurate. To attempt to disguise aspects of the program that are weak is not only dishonest, but also may result in a short term hire. Candor is best for everyone. If weak areas are present (and every school has them), admit it and challenge the prospective teacher to consider being a part of the team to make these areas stronger in the future.

Aggressively follow up

Finally, aggressively follow up any good prospects. The most effective recruiters are those with an effective follow-up system in place. Letters, emails and telephone calls communicate your interest to the sharper candidates. Everyone wants to be wanted, and this strategy brings results.

In this first stage the administrator and the college student get to know each other. The administrator is noting the teaching fields, personality, and character of the student. At the same time, the student is evaluating whether this is the kind of ministry that is right for him or her. The administrator enthusiastically presents the mission and distinctives of the Christian school, and those factors resonate with likeminded young people.

Stage Two: Mutual Evaluation

When both the administrator and the prospective teacher are interested, the second stage of the hiring procedure begins. The school has a need and the prospective teacher fits in with the culture of the school. There have been no red flags observed by either party—no practical or philosophical issues which would prohibit taking the discussion further. At this second stage, mutual evaluation, most of the important issues are discussed. This discussion could occur on campus or by telephone.

Getting to know the individual

After general, friendly greetings, transition into getting to know the applicant as a whole person. The following may be important:

- If the applicant is married ask
  - How long have you been married?
  - Is this the only marriage for each of you?
  - Children? (ages, special needs, grades, status in school—academically and behaviorally)
- Ask about directed teaching (student teaching) experience or past teaching experience:
  - What did you enjoy most in the student teaching?
  - What area(s) did you enjoy the least? Why?
  - What did you learn from the experience?
  - Were you surprised about any aspect of the teaching experience? If so what was it?
  - What would you change about the teaching experience?
  - What grade did you make? Did you feel that the grade was warranted? Why or why not?
- When did you believe that God had called you to the ministry of Christian school teaching? Listen to the story.
- What are your long-term ministry goals? (Administration? College teaching? Mission field? Other?)

Do not be locked into these questions. Be ready especially to follow the discussion in new directions that may be suggested by the answer to any question. This is important throughout the interview.

Salvation and call-to-the-ministry testimony

The administrator should not make assumptions here. One of the important elements in selecting a Christlike faculty is a clear testimony from the prospective teacher. This aspect of the interview is enjoyable fellowship, and it reassures both the administrator and the prospective teacher. It reassures the administrator that this is the right teacher, and it reassures the prospective teacher that he or she is going to a school where spiritual essentials are important.

Philosophy of education

The administrator should seek to determine the educational philosophy of the applicant. First the administrator asks the prospective teacher questions to learn about that person's key beliefs. After that the administrator should freely share his own philosophy of education. Again, it is important to be clear with the applicant. In order to be most effective in the ministry of Christian education, the Christian school should be comprised of a faculty with a similar philosophy of education.

Asking yes-or-no questions, such as "Do you believe the Bible is the Word of God?" results in the administrator leading the conversation. Open-ended questions, such as "What do you believe the Bible to be?" allow a candidate to reveal more of his actual beliefs. The following are some possible questions:

- Why do you want to teach in a Christian school rather than in a secular school?
- What is the goal of Christian education?
- Describe to me what you would count as success after a student has been through your class.
- Who should attend a Christian school?
    - Follow-up: Is there room for accepting unsaved students?
    - Follow-up: How much do the parents have to be in agreement with the spiritual and behavioral standards?

- What do you do if a student is in violation of a school standard, listening to worldly music outside of school, for example?
- What colleges would you recommend? Why?
- What kind of church would you choose to attend?
- If the teacher is an unmarried college student, ask about the relationship with his or her with parents.

The disciplinary system

There must be an agreement between the administrator and the applicant about the roles played by the faculty and the administrator in the discipline system. The administrator should ask how the applicant has handled specific incidents in previous teaching experience. For the first-year teacher, of course, directed teaching is that previous experience, and that is expected to be a learning time. The administrator should explain how the system operates at his or her school. How, when, and how often are disciplinary procedures utilized? What support is available from the administration, and how does the teacher seek that help? A thorough discussion of this facet of the school program is critical to give the prospective teacher confidence. It is important to be frank about this because at the next stage, the visit, the discerning applicant will recognize any inconsistencies.

Church membership expectations

If the school is a ministry of a local church and there is a church membership requirement, the administrator must be clear about that and provide information about the church ministry. What opportunities will be available to the teacher in the local church? Are there specific church attendance requirements? What accountability programs, if any, are in place? These expectations should be understood in advance of a formal visit and interview.

Employee standards and expectations

All expectations and standards should be clear to the candidate well in advance of the presentation of a contract. Standards and expectations should be clearly expressed, even before a visit. If all of the expectations are laid out in a faculty manual (as they should be), a copy should be provided to the candidate in advance of a telephone conversation or an interview at the college.

Written job description

In addition to the employee standards and expectations, the candidate should understand clearly what the job includes. Whenever possible, a written description of the responsibilities should be provided for the candidate to study in advance of a conversation with the administrator. This job description should include all extra duties and responsibilities that are expected of teachers. If there are some extra duties that are unknown at the time of the interview, the administrator should be clear about the possibility of the faculty member receiving additional duties and the process that would be followed in making the decision.

Facility strengths and limitations

One of the reasons for the personal visit is to provide the candidate with an opportunity to assess the building and resources available and to consider how he or she can serve, given the circumstances God has provided. Information given in advance of the visit will be very helpful for the candidate. Positive but honest presentation of these details helps the new teacher have confidence in the administrator. Surprises erode confidence.

Support level

The salary and benefit structure should be clearly provided to the candidate at this stage. The expense of a visit to the ministry is unnecessary if it would be impossible for the candidate to work at the school for any reason.

References

The administrator should ask for a list of references, including address, telephone, and email for each. Each of the following people can provide pertinent insights:

- The applicant's home pastor
- A college professor
- The supervising teacher from directed teaching or the college instructor who supervises student teachers
- An employer

Do not hesitate to ask for these or other specific references. The administrator may give the applicant a form with these categories on it, leaving blanks for others that the applicant would like to include.

A prospective teacher's references should be consulted in advance of a visit. Unfortunately, this research is one of the most neglected aspects of the hiring process. While the wise administrator will be very proactive and aggressive in teacher recruitment, he or she must be equally vigilant in the interview and reference stage. Hiring an ineffective teacher or one who does not fit well with the philosophy of the ministry will do great harm to the confidence that the parents, students, and faculty have in the school and in the administrator. The administrator should check with the references to evaluate the applicant's training and experience in teaching as well as spiritual and character matters.

Contact the references by telephone or in writing. Asking the following questions should reveal something about the spiritual growth and faithfulness of the applicant:[8]

- Has the applicant been faithful to church?
- Has the applicant been involved in personal evangelism or

---

8   Several items from this list were drawn from Dan Burrell, Phillip Johnson, and Paul Tatham, *Perspectives in Christian Education: Focus on Parent and Student Relationships*, p. 39.

discipleship?

- Does the applicant demonstrate a love for students?
- Does the applicant show warmth?
- Is the applicant a worthy Christian role model?
- Is the applicant enthusiastic?
- Is the applicant courteous?
- Is the applicant emotionally healthy?
- Has the applicant been involved in teaching in the church or in other areas of ministry?
- Is the applicant growing in his or her Christian walk?
- Has the applicant been involved in other ministry opportunities such as Christian summer camps or short-term missions work in the past few years?
- If you had a child in our school, would you want this person to be his or her teacher?

The answers to these questions should begin to provide the information that is necessary to determine whether the applicant is a Christlike example now, and it will help to predict his or her future level of ministry commitment.

Open and honest communication is essential throughout the evaluation phase. This kind of communication will be respected and appreciated by the candidate.

Stage Three: The Visit to the Hiring School

The third and final stage of the process should be the visit of the applicant to the school and, if applicable, to the sponsoring church. By this point the administrator and teacher candidate now have a good understanding of each other. All questions have been answered, all references have been checked carefully, and both parties are prepared to sign the contract unless there is a surprise discovered on the visit. This visit should be a required part of the hiring process. The expenses should be paid by the school. Meals and housing during the visit could be in the home of a member of the administrative staff or a faculty member with whom the teacher will work closely. Obviously, there are advantages beyond the financial to this housing-and-meals arrangement. The extended contact provides more time for the prospective teacher to interact with quality staff in both formal and informal settings. The hosts become another source of insights about the ministry for the candidate: they will very likely have occasion to present the joys of ministry in general and the value of serving at this school in particular. The administrator can also gain insights from the hosts about their impression of the candidate and his or her reaction to the administrator and school.

Interviews should be scheduled with the pastor, administrator, and, perhaps, other administrative staff members. Anyone to whom the teacher will answer should be scheduled for an interview. Those involved should be encouraged to ask all appropriate questions to discern a successful match of philosophy and practice.

Every effort should be made to allow the candidate to see things as they really are within the school. Again, disguising weak areas may result in the instability of a one-year stay, followed by starting the recruitment process over. The administrator must be committed to the long-term development of the staff, students, and facilities, all to God's glory.

Before, during, and after the hiring process, the Christian school leaders must be praying. They need to seek God's direction about what their real needs are as well as how to meet them. "Man's goings are of the LORD; how can a man then understand his own way?" (Proverbs 20:24)

Prayer and diligence are the keys to selecting a Christ-honoring faculty. If the administrator is effective in hiring competent, godly, and dedicated people, many of the problems that dominate so much of his time will be remedied or reduced. Good people make a good school.

Note

Our focus has been on the selection of personnel as it relates to developing Christlikeness in students through the Christian school. Every detail of the hiring process has potential to affect the ability of the school to accomplish its main purpose. The following two sources go into more detail on the hiring process:

- *Some Light on Christian Education*, James Deuink, Ed. Chapter 10, "Selecting the School Administrator"; and Chapter 11, "Developing a Qualified Professional Staff."
- *Effective Christian School Management*, James Deuink and Carl Herbster. Chapter 8, "Selecting and Recruiting Personnel."

References

Deuink, J. W., & Herbster, C. D. (n.d.). *Effective Christian school management.* Greenville, SC: Bob Jones University.

Burrell, D., Johnson, P., & Tatham, P. (1991). *Perspectives in Christian education: Focus on parent and student relationships.* Enumclaw, WA: WinePress Publishing.

Deuink, J. (Ed.). (1984). *Some light on Christian education.* Greenville, SC: Bob Jones University.

Developing a Christ-honoring Faculty

The administrator as a discipler of faculty

One of the most important responsibilities of a Christian school administrator is the development of a quality, committed, Christ-honoring faculty. The administrator who recognizes the importance and challenge of this responsibility and has totally committed himself to the task has made a good start. Long-term commitment to this goal is also required to have a school marked by excellence in Christlike character and in every aspect of learning.

Once the faculty team is in place, the administrator must disciple and support them. This process never ends. The wise administrator will constantly be looking for ways to effectively meet the needs of the faculty. The needs of the veteran teacher are obviously different from those of the first-year teacher. The veteran teacher who is new to your school presents another set of opportunities. The key is to develop general programs and procedures that will assist every faculty member while keeping an eye out for special needs. The administrator must approach every relationship with the heart of a discipler.

Great balance is needed if the administrator is to disciple his staff. Strong leadership and humility are equally essential. As the administrator encourages the staff to model the fruit of the Holy Spirit (Galatians 5:22-23) to the students, the administrator models the same character qualities for the staff. The administrator must be growing in his own walk with God, because no one can lead another where he himself is not going.

The Local Church: Personal Development

Local church involvement is important for the spiritual growth of any Christian. The contract for staff members and the ministry policy manual should require active involvement in a good church as a condition of employment. If the school is part of one local church or is sponsored by one church, it is reasonable that attendance at that particular church should be required of all *full-time* faculty and staff. Hearing the same messages from the same pastor promotes the development of unity in philosophy and vision for the ministry as a whole.

The teacher will receive exhortation and encouragement from the church in many ways, the foremost being the preaching service. Although serving in the local church is critical for the faculty member, he or she should not miss all the preaching services by serving elsewhere in the church. There is no substitute for being under the good, solid preaching of God's Word to keep life in the proper perspective and to keep one's relationship with the Lord right.

The teacher must be faithful to all the regular services of his or her church, but the Sunday school plays a special role. It is important for the new faculty member to establish friendships within the church, and one of the most effective ways to accomplish this is through a Sunday school class. The new teacher must have balance. There may be a temptation to work 24/7 to accomplish the many tasks of Christian education. Working to exhaustion or social isolation may even sound noble, but the temptation must be resisted in favor of a more balanced approach. Balanced people are better teachers. Teachers must be relational. One part of maintaining this side of healthy personhood is to be involved in the social and recreational fellowship provided through the Sunday school program. Encouraging this level of participation will assist the administrator in the development of his staff.

Some churches may have additional programs in place that can be helpful for the Christian school teacher. There may be a ladies' ministry, a men's ministry, a small-group program, or other opportunities. The teacher should consider each of these programs. In many churches, there is so much going on that a faculty member will be unable to participate in all of the activities. However, the teacher should give prayerful consideration to what is necessary to be an integral part of the church. Active local church involvement will greatly assist the faculty member to keep life—and teaching—fresh and exciting.

The model teacher actively serves in the local church. Some of this service is within the church, such as singing in the choir or teaching in a children's ministry. Outreach is also important. The teacher must model this as well. Many churches have bus ministries, and most have visitation ministries. When the time pressure hits, outreach opportunities are often the first commitments to be dropped. Yet, every Christian has the responsibility of evangelism.

Granted, the teacher has been serving God in the classroom all day. Yet other church members have been working at their secular jobs all day too, and they serve in the church beyond that. The teacher should go beyond his or her paid employment in serving in the local church. Ministry service beyond the paid duties is not just a good example; it is essential to the spiritual growth of any teacher or administrator.

Yet, there is the reality of time. The preaching and teaching of the Word, fellowship, Christian service—all are important. But they take time. The professional ministry of teaching also demands much time. Balance is the key. Especially when entering a new church, the teacher should commit carefully, and not hastily. Commit carefully, but commit faithfully!

The support of the school staff for the church must be obvious to all. There must be consistent church attendance, visitation, and tithing. If these characteristics have already been a pattern in the teachers' lives prior to being hired, they are likely to continue. The apostle Paul sums up this dynamic balance of God's working in him as he, Paul, works in others: "Warning every man, and teaching every man in all wisdom; that we may present every man perfect in Christ Jesus: Whereunto I also labour, striving according to his working, which worketh in me mightily" (Colossians 1:28-29). The desire must be to labor—*the teacher's work in the students' lives*—as Christ works mightily in the teacher—*God's work in the teacher's life*. If the Christian school is to produce mature students and graduates that are testimonies of God's grace and goodness, each staff member must be faithful in his or her own walk with the Lord. "The servant is not greater than his lord; neither is he that is sent greater than he that sent him" (John 13:16).

The administrator's task of developing a Christ-honoring faculty will be easier if teachers are actively involved in a local church or churches. Each teachers should love his or her church. Teachers should allow others to minister to them and should allow the Holy Spirit to minister through them to others.

The School: Professional Development

The administrator also has a responsibility to assist the spiritual *and* professional growth of each faculty member within the framework of the school. Special attention must be paid to the newest teachers. Yet, the veteran teachers are still growing too and have their distinctive needs. A thoughtful set of programs reflects both big-picture planning and flexibility to meet the range of needs.

New Teacher Orientation

The fears of anxious new teachers are greatly calmed by organized, active support demonstrated at the very outset of their ministry. An in-service time especially for new teachers should include aspects of the ministry that will provide them with practical information as they begin the year. Workshops could include the following:

- A historical perspective of the school and, if applicable, the sponsoring church
- Guidelines for classroom management;
- Procedures for requesting copies or instruction in working the copier;
- Procedures for requisitioning supplies or classroom repairs;
- Grading scale and grades management, especially if a school-wide computer grading program is used.

These topics may be unnecessary for the veteran teacher, but they are extremely valuable to the new teacher. These sessions should include devotional insights and a vision for the future of the ministry.

New Teacher Support

The administrator can make or break the young teacher. The investment of significant time in the teacher during the first year or two will repay the administrator bountifully in the years to come. The new faculty member needs a secure, stable, and organized environment. The professional and spiritual tone of this environment is established by an administrator who is growing in his or her own walk with the Lord, is consistent in decision making, and is balanced in personal and professional life. The discipling administrator is committed to developing Christlike teachers and students and to excellence in every endeavor of the school. Observing the administrator, the new teacher should be inspired to live the Ecclesiastes 9:10 life: "Whatsoever thy hand findeth to do, do it with thy might."

The whole faculty should support the new teacher. The veteran teachers can show how the philosophy of the school and the expectations of the leadership should be manifested in daily life. The new teacher sees the loving support of peers in prayer meetings, in break room fellowship, and, perhaps, in mentor-teacher support. Each member of the faculty and staff should possess the heart of a discipler, with the administrator setting the pace by his example and his expectations.

Teacher Mentoring

Some things are caught far better than taught. A college course in professional communication is valuable, but for a new teacher to see and hear the veteran take control of an excited group of fifth graders is above valuation. The supervised teaching semester of the college days is valuable, but it does not complete the transition. The mentor teacher helps the new teacher complete the change from college theory to classroom practice, especially regarding the philosophy and culture of the new school.

The teacher mentoring program has advantages for all involved. The mentor sharpens his or her own skills by thinking through how to help the protégé. There is also a deep satisfaction in helping another teacher get off to a good start. The new teacher not only gains practical tips and insights, but also gains a friend. In the stressful life of a teacher, especially when every problem is a new problem, there is great strength in the fellowship of the ministry. One of the best facilitators of growth for the experienced teacher is a role in assisting the administrator's work with new teachers. The administrator gains greatly too. The mentor teacher and the new teacher both are encouraged and become stronger. Mentoring also improves staff retention. Studies have shown that teachers who are mentored are less likely to become discouraged and drop out of teaching after the first year. A *Journal for Christian Educators* article, "Teacher Mentoring," explores this topic in more detail (Krueger, 2005).

Quality In-service Training Program

Each school year begins with time to consider and discuss practical and philosophical matters. Beginning the teachers' paid work time a week before the first day of classes allows time for these sessions and time for other preparations for the new school year. These other duties may involve tasks in which the teachers help with final building preparations, and should certainly include time for the teachers to prepare for their own classroom teaching.

Veterans and new teachers alike benefit from on-going training. The administrator will plan, organize, lead, and teach, but the administrator does not need to teach it all. Other staff members can benefit from preparing and leading parts of the program. A well-planned, quality in-service training program helps in the development of a Christ-honoring faculty.

Much consideration must be given to every aspect of the program's training and personal enrichment elements so that this will be an effective time. Topics to consider as a part of this training include the following:

- Philosophy
- Curriculum development
- Materials and methods
- Spiritual growth and development of students and faculty
- Inspirational workshops/sermons
- Motivational workshops/sermons
- Dealing appropriately with parents
- Dealing appropriately with students
- Appropriate handling of the textbooks and materials
- Appropriate handling of technology
- The learning levels in the classroom
- The varying learning styles in the classroom
- The able learner
- The struggling learner
- Personal life, budgeting, and saving as a Christian teacher

Obviously this list is only a representative sampling of topics. Every day should also include something from the Word of God. As with the professional sessions, the administrator can share with others the opportunities to present these devotionals. Anything communicated as a devotional or Bible challenge must be fresh from the presenter's own walk with the Lord.

Plan the program carefully. Do not approach this or any important area in a haphazard way.

Individual Discipleship by the Administrator

What an encouragement it is to a teacher to recognize that the busy administrator is concerned for him or her! Do whatever it takes to make time for individual meetings with each teacher regularly. These conferences could occur as often as a weekly touch-base time or as little as a monthly meeting. The key is for the administrator to live the life of a discipler. You must maintain emphasis on staff development and spiritual growth. The investment of your life in the lives of the staff will provide immediate results and eternal benefits.

Disciplinary Support

A good, experienced teacher will not often need help with classroom discipline; but new teachers often will, and it is important for all teachers at times. A powerful source of discouragement to teachers is the administrator's failure to support them in handling disciplinary issues. If a teacher becomes discouraged or frustrated, Satan has his foot in the door, and great damage is possible. The wise administrator will be aware of this need and will guide and support the teachers.

Informal Faculty Observation Programs

MBWA Program. The Management-by-Walking-Around philosophy is certainly the most effective approach to school leadership. Many administrators sit behind their desks all day except for teaching an occasional class. Regularly walking through the school allows you to have a finger on the pulse of the school. It is essential to your reaching maximum effectiveness in leading your school. You can learn much by simply standing in the hallway, eating lunch in the cafeteria, or casually making the rounds of the faculty before and after school. Your goal is to make some brief contact every day with every staff member and many students.

Informal Observation. The administrator or someone on the administrative team should make this observation. It should take approximately ten minutes and should be accompanied by either a brief conversation with the faculty member about what was observed or a brief written report. Informal observations, taking place weekly, greatly enhance the administrator's understanding of the teachers and students.

Mentor-Teacher Observation. The purpose of this observation is to give the mentor teacher an opportunity to provide encouragement and assistance to the younger teacher. Every attempt should be made to ensure that this observation is a very positive experience. The mentor teacher, although not the new teacher's boss, will be able to provide many good ideas. The new teacher can also be freed up to observe the mentor teacher. The investment required to allow time for these observations will bring valuable results to both of these teachers and to the school.

Collegial Observation. This observation is entirely at the request of a teacher, but the administrator should let teachers know that it is something they may request. A teacher will ask a colleague to come and observe some specific areas of his or her teaching during a 30-minute time frame. The colleague makes notes and provides them to the one observed.

Observe a Teacher in a Sister School. It is good to develop relationships with other biblically sound Christian schools. Permission must be sought between administrators, but release time should be granted to teachers who desire to grow by observing other teachers.

Formal Faculty Observations

You will get not what you expect, but what you inspect. If you expect your faculty to maintain Christ-honoring educational professionalism, you must inspect it. At least once a year each teacher, including the administrator if he or she teaches, should have a formal observation. The administrator who does this organized observation can speak with authority and specific detail when asked about the quality of the school's teaching staff. Formal observations allow the opportunity to see and meet needs as well. This positive pressure is also good for the teacher. Good teachers rise to the challenge.

Preobservation conference. This meeting, which should last 30-45 minutes, accomplishes two major things. First, the administrator conveys his intent to be positive and helpful, an ally in the process of professional growth. Second, the administrator can clarify what he or she is looking for and answer any questions. The teacher is provided with a copy of the observation instrument before this conference. For the new teacher, the preobservation conference provides answers about how the form is filled out as well as about the administrator's expectations. For the veteran teacher, a look at the most recent observation is a reminder of what the administrator is looking for in the next observation. In either case this is a time for discipling the teacher. This conference should be very positive and instructive, while also clarifying expectations and accountability.

It is possible to review the observation process with the whole staff as a group. This, of course, saves time. There are advantages to both methods.

Observation. This observation should encompass an entire class period (secondary) or lesson (elementary). It should include the beginning and ending transitions. There are many instruments that could be used by the administrator to record observation notes. Attention to detail is important in a formal observation such as this one. Many positive things should be noted, as well as a few comments that could help the teacher improve. Try for a five-to-one encouragement ratio. If many problems are observed, the administrator should exercise wisdom by pointing out only the most important ones to work on until the next observation. The goal is progress, not devastation.

After-observation Conference. The after-observation conference should be scheduled within a few days of the observation. It should include encouraging comments, general observations, and instructive suggestions. This conference can be a very valuable discipleship time. The administrator must assist the faculty member in becoming all that he or she can be! The observation instrument should include a place for the administrator's signature, the teacher's signature, and the date of the observation. The teacher should be given a copy of the completed and signed document, and the original should go in the teacher's file in the administrator's office. If consideration must be given to replacing a faculty member, this paper trail is a necessary part of determining whether or not the teacher is making progress.

Quality Outside Training

Take advantage of opportunities available to assist the faculty in their development process. Opportunities are available in most areas of the country. Membership in state, regional, or national Christian school organizations opens many more opportunities.

- Conferences
    - State and regional educators' conferences
    - National educators' conferences
- On-site evaluation
    - Well-qualified educational consultants
    - School improvement program
    - Accreditation program
- Professional development resources
    - Professional journals for teachers and administrators
    - Books with a Christian perspective
    - Training videos

The administrator, as the leader of the school, must possess a deep desire to grow and must provide the instruction and motivation for the faculty also to develop. The administrator should encourage the faculty to pursue advanced degrees from quality Christian colleges that support the mission of the school. Taking your teachers to a state or regional Christian educators' conference is a top priority. It is one of the highlights of the year for teachers and administrators alike. This time away provides physical and spiritual refreshment. Interacting with colleagues gives ideas and inspiration to carry back to the home school. Yes, it is a budget challenge, but it must be a priority if you are to lead a growing staff.

Faculty Development: Much to Gain . . . and Lose

"Leadership is influence, . . . the ability to move another person in a direction you believe is important" (Collier & Williams, p. 1). In order to influence most effectively in the Christian school, you should not only publicly cast the vision, but also you should privately disciple, mentor, and encourage the faculty. Teachers must recognize that the administrator cares about every aspect of their lives. As they do, the ministry of the administrator to the students and their families is multiplied through teachers who have made the school's mission their own. The development of a positive, energetic, and spiritual atmosphere among the faculty is a time-consuming process, but it is the most important task of the administrator.

Sometimes the difficult decision must be made to release a faculty member because of spiritual problems or a lack of professional competence. If you ever must do this, you will want to know that you have courageously and consistently done everything possible to help that teacher.

When the Christian school movement began, there were faculty members who sacrificed much to have the privilege of ministry to the children. Much progress has been made in pay scales and facilities, but Christian educators must not lose the ministry attitude, which is the heartbeat of the movement! They must dedicate themselves to pleasing God with their lives and ask Him to use them to make an eternal difference in the lives of the young people. Faculty development is important to providing the best in Christian education

Administrator, as you continue to pursue excellence in every area of the Christian school, do not settle for less than God's best in your faculty. Pray, preach, and teach. Spend individual time developing the teachers in your care. You, and they, must understand the expectation that God has for those of us involved in ministry: "My brethren, be not many masters, knowing that we shall receive the greater condemnation" (James 3:1).

God can give you the wisdom to lead in the development of a competent, Christ-honoring faculty.

References

Collier, K., & Williams, M. (2004). *Biblical leadership*. Greenville, SC: Ambassador Emerald International.

Krueger, C. (2005, spring). Teacher mentoring. *Christian Educators Journal, 11* (2), 18-21.

A Culture of Discipleship
Administration, staff, and students

Who is shaping the spiritual atmosphere of your school? If you do not know, it is imperative that you find out. The spiritual quality of a school should not be directed by whichever students happen to be most influential and outspoken. You should be—and can be—the one who sets the pace. By implementing biblical principles of discipleship, the administrator can work through the staff to set the direction for the student body.

An effective leader is first of all a discipler. Again, leadership is the ability to influence people in a direction that you think is important. Christian leadership is all about helping others to develop Christlike attitudes. Who is changing for the Lord because of your influence? Over the years, your job titles may change and the tasks may shift; but the only thing that really changes is the group of individuals that you enjoy the privilege of discipling. The administrator must possess the heart of a discipler if a positive spiritual atmosphere is to prevail in the school.

In order to establish and maintain a Christlike atmosphere in your school, each member of the school faculty must be a disciple-maker. This focus on discipleship must begin with the administrator, flow to the faculty, and then extend to the young people who have a heart for God. Unfortunately, too many administrators view their jobs as task-oriented instead of people-oriented. They are more focused on the *things* to do than on the *people* who do them.

The Need for Radical Change in Focus

"Teachers tend to teach as they were taught," and administrators tend to administrate as those before them. The many necessary tasks of administration—things like budgets, programs, and class assignments—can obscure the basic mission of the Christian school administrator: to lead in the development of Christlike character. The problem is that everyone is a sinner. That truth matters in the school as much as in the church. Administrators are using an unbiblical model of educational leadership if they take their eyes off the fact that depravity is a reality and that salvation and discipleship are necessary elements of God's remedy. Without a conscious focus on the development of Christlike character, the administrator misses one of the tremendous privileges and joys of his or her calling. "Education without God's Word makes men clever devils." Even Christian schools will descend into making "clever devils" if they lose sight of the real goal.

The goal of deliberate discipleship is primary. Educators can get too focused on education. That may sound ridiculous to educators who are not gripped by a passion for truly Christian education. The Bible says, "Be not wise in thine own eyes, fear the Lord, and depart from evil" (Proverbs 3:7). Even though the administrator is saved by grace, the natural tendency persists to rely on one's own wisdom and the wisdom of the world. Yes, the school must tend to its distinct mission, education. But administrators should tend to it with the overall goal in mind, and God is clear about

His goal: "For whom he did foreknow, he also did predestinate to be conformed to the image of his Son" (Romans 8:29).

The problem of man's basic sin nature is compounded by another problem: few administrators have enjoyed the privilege of being mentored or discipled by someone who selflessly invested his or her life in that task. Therefore, they have followed an administrative model copied from the public school. True, most public school administrators care about good citizenship and character, and there are many effective school management ideas to be learned from secular educators. The basic purpose of Christian education is different, though. It is not just good academics with the add-on feature of biblical perspective. The radical difference of Christian education is that all of the academic excellence—which must not be neglected—is just part of the main goal, the development of Christlike character to the glory of God.

The goal is to change people, but there is just one problem: the administrator can't do it. Granted, a few people have a natural talent for influencing others, but any lasting spiritual work must be done by God. He has called all Christians, not just the naturally talented, to be His servants in that task (Matthew 28:19-20). God has also provided all of the necessary means, the most important being prayer. "With men it is impossible, but not with God: for with God all things are possible" (Mark 10:27). The administrator must do all that he or she can, balancing action with earnest prayer for God's working in the lives of individuals in the school. The Lord Jesus put it succinctly: "For without me ye can do nothing" (John 15:5).

If the administrator is an effective discipler, the faculty and staff will become effective disciplers. As the faculty and staff become effective, the godly student leaders will have a biblical model to follow and will more effectively influence their peers and the atmosphere of the school. As the school atmosphere is changed, the schedule of the administrator will be freed up to become more involved in discipleship. Talk about an upward spiral!

Missionary Warren Webster said, "If I had my life to live over again, I would live it to change the lives of people, because you have not changed anything until you've changed the lives of people."

The Pattern of Discipleship [9]

The Mindset of the Discipler[10]

The model that Christ provided is multifaceted, but one of its most outstanding—and surprising—qualities is humility.

"Ye know that they which are accounted to rule over the Gentiles exercise lordship over them; and their great ones exercise authority upon them. But so shall it not be among you: but whosoever will be great among you, shall be your minister: And whosoever of you will be the chiefest, shall be servant of all. *For even the Son of man came not to be ministered unto, but to minister, and to give his life a ransom for many.*" (Mark 10:42-45) Humility is the attitude of a servant. The Lord of Lords and King of Kings knelt and washed the disciples' feet, thus modeling God's view of leadership. What a humbling but perfect example He was for the disciples then and for any Christian leader today. If the Lord of Glory could humble Himself as a servant, how much more should that humility permeate Christian school leadership?

Jesus served at the least convenient times. He washed the disciple's feet on the evening of his betrayal, just before the Cross (John 13:3-5, 12-17). When the pressures were great upon Him (is pressure familiar, you who lead in Christian work?) Christ kept His focus on serving. When others should have been serving, comforting, and supporting Him, Christ knelt at the disciples'

---

9   For an excellent discussion on discipleship, read John Goetsch and Mark Rasmussen's *Mentoring and Modeling,* Lancaster, CA: Revival Books.

10   Much of the content of this section is borrowed from Dr. John Monroe.

feet with a towel and a wash bowl and modeled His expectations for those who would lead in His kingdom. Are administrators too position-conscious to humble themselves? What an example Christ provided!

The leader will manifest the attitude of humility in myriad actions, both tender and tough. The Apostle Paul was a remarkable leader. God used him, in just two or three weeks time, to win many souls to Christ in Thessalonica and to establish a new church. After being driven out of town, he wrote back to instruct, exhort, and encourage—things disciple makers do. Reflecting on his time there, he gives a rare insight into his method of ministry:

> But we were gentle among you, even as a nurse cherisheth her children: So being affectionately desirous of you, we were willing to have imparted unto you, not the gospel of God only, but also our own souls, because ye were dear unto us. For ye remember, brethren, our labour and travail: for labouring night and day, because we would not be chargeable unto any of you, we preached unto you the gospel of God. (1 Thessalonians 2:7-9)

We were gentle. The Greek verb is passive voice: *we were made gentle.* This is a work that God does in you. You cannot maintain this attitude without the supernatural action of the Holy Spirit. The word *gentle* is potent too: "mild in bearing with the faults of others; one, too, who is gentle (though firm) in reproving the erroneous opinions of others" (Jameison, Faussett, and Brown). Your discipling will probably involve moments when you bear the faults of the faculty or students you disciple, perhaps in how they treat you or in helping to repair their mistakes in dealing with others. You will have to be gentle and firm in "reproving …

erroneous opinions"—in helping people see their problems and opportunities God's way.

The tenderness of a *nurse*, that is, a nursing mother, is described in verse seven. This pictures one selflessly meeting needs, as a mother cares for her child's health and welfare. How many of school administrators are examples of this type of commitment?

Although all educators fail to some degree, all must recognize their need to develop this type of relationship with faculty members while encouraging them to do the same with their students. A truly Christlike atmosphere will occur only as leaders follow Christ's model.

This picture of motherly concern implies a foundational responsibility. A mother must take care of herself in order to effectively take care of her baby. The leader must be strong in the Lord. The passage goes on to say, "Ye are witnesses, and God also, how *holily* and *justly* and *unblameably* we behaved ourselves among you that believe" (1 Thessalonians 2:10). Administrators must be growing and changing if they are to properly lead others. They must be strong in their walk with the Lord if they are to be effective in discipleship of others. They must present an example that is Christlike as they invest their lives in the lives of others

After the tenderness of a mother is discussed in verses 7-9, the leadership of a loving father is described in verses 11-12:

> As ye know how we exhorted and comforted and charged every one of you, as a father doth his children, That ye would walk worthy of God, who hath called you unto his kingdom and glory. For this cause also thank we God without ceasing, because, when ye received the word of God which ye heard of us, ye received it not as the word of men, but as it is in truth, the word of God, which effectually worketh also in you that believe. (1 Thessalonians 2:11-13)

The effective discipler communicates more than tenderness, care, and concern. The job description goes beyond modeling selflessness. The effective discipler also provides the leadership that the one being discipled needs.

This leadership is manifested in three ways in this passage:

- *Exhort*—"to call to one's side, to instruct"
- *Comfort*—"to calm and console, to encourage"
- *Charge*—"to bear witness, i.e. to affirm that one has seen or heard or experienced something" (Strong)

When a faculty member needs encouragement or needs strength for the burdens of teaching, you must be ready to *exhort*. Exhortation involves instruction, telling what to do. Interestingly, the Greek word is *parakaleo*, one of the words used to describe the role of the Holy Spirit as the One called alongside to help. It is critical that you be strong enough to provide direction when faculty members need it. Warning may be in order, and you must be secure enough in your walk with the Lord to provide that challenge.

A faculty member may need *comfort* in a difficult time. Instruction teaches the intellect, but comfort touches the heart. If comfort is needed, you must be there. A telephone call or note, while good, is probably not all that is needed. One of the highest comments of praise from teens is "He was there for me." The word *there* in that phrase speaks of the basic human need of proximity.

Perhaps the idea of *charge*, as it relates to bearing witness, is the appeal to the will. The Greek is the word also translated *martyr*, suggesting that the one doing the exhortation has been faithful through the worst of times, and has seen God's faithfulness triumph. To *charge* is to say, "Hang in there. I've been there, and I have seen that the grace of God is always sufficient."

What a wonderful balance is seen in the tenderness of a mother and the strength of a father! What an example! The admonition that is given in this passage should be the consistent focus of discipleship in a Christian school. There need not be an official "program" in place, but the heart, spirit, and mentality of discipleship must permeate the culture of the school.

Whom to Disciple

Christ was certainly connected with His disciples. He invested substantial time and effort in them, especially with the inner circle: Peter, James, and John. Jesus recognized that His work with them would be multiplied in the years to come by their ministries and by the ministry that each of *their* discipled converts would carry yet further.

Similarly, each Christian school leader must disciple the staff, who will multiply that discipleship ministry and carry it on. The focus of discipleship is others-oriented. It is built on relationships and is very interested in one product: spiritual growth.

Systematic, long-term discipleship of students by teachers is rare. True, godly teachers naturally encourage and exhort students, but discipleship is not common. One reason is that faculty members are not being effectively discipled by administrators. The goal is to develop a strong staff so that every teacher disciples his or her own students. Certain issues will always require action by the administrator. Yet, as faculty leadership is developed, many of the issues that now demand administrative intervention may be handled in a Christlike way by the mature faculty. Furthermore, a culture of discipleship reduces discipline problems. The time that the administrator must spend on handling disciplinary problems will decrease significantly. Better discipleship leads eventually to fewer discipline problems, allowing the administrator more time to disciple both faculty and students.

In a small school, the administrator may be able to disciple each teacher. In a large school the administrator must work with the key leaders of his staff. Make a distinction, though, between people who lead and leadership positions. Certain positions carry more opportunities for discipleship than others. Positions of greater influence include the administrative staff, academic department heads, coaches, music director, drama director, or senior class advisor. Regardless of the size of school, people holding leadership positions should be growing and discipling others as a result of the administrator's investment in their lives. If faculty or staff members, especially those in leadership positions, do not eventually accept and implement this vision, staff changes may be in order. The leadership of the school must follow the biblical model. Those in leadership positions must be committed to investing their lives in the lives of the students.

The faculty positions having the greatest influence on students and other faculty must be the focus of the more in-depth discipleship by the administrator. However, the administrator must be careful to avoid any perception of favoritism toward particular faculty members. The key faculty members either must already be in the positions of leadership, justifying greater discipleship by the administrator, or they should be moved into them. The Christlike development of each of these leaders will magnify the impact of the discipling administrator.

As you spend substantial time with key people on the faculty, changes will come. Sometimes these changes come very naturally. However, you will sometimes have the responsibility to confront individuals over actions and attitudes needing change. No administrator enjoys the meetings in which confrontation takes place, but these are crucial to effectively leading a school. The administrator will, at times need to delineate clear changes that must take place in the life of a staff member, and maybe even the time frame in which those changes must take place. The key to this type of meeting is to have previously established a caring relationship with the teacher, the "nurturing mother" side of 1 Thessalonians chapter 2. The teacher must know that the administrator cares on a personal level and that the administrator wants him or her to succeed. If the administrator leads with the heart of a humble servant of the Lord, being transparent about his or her own past mistakes and current change points, it is much easier for others to accept correction and direction. When faculty members can clearly see the administrator's earnest desire to do them good, they more readily accept correction.

Again, you can't, but God can: pray. However, you have a role to play in God's plan. Keep the balance: pray and act.

Getting Started

First, decide who are the key people for discipling students or other staff members. Next, set up a weekly time with each of them. It is possible to combine some in groups, but the group setting will diminish the benefits and may restrict how frankly other people's struggles may be discussed. The meeting must allow candor in addressing struggles faced by the one whom you are discipling. A discussion of the staff member's discipleship ministry must also be a part of each meeting. There will be many practical but unrelated items to cover in these regular meetings, such as schedules or budgets, but the discussion must focus on spiritual growth, first in the life of the staff member you are discipling and then in the lives of those for whom that person is responsible. Last, schedule time to be with key student leaders. Student council meetings could provide some of this time, but one-on-one time has special value. Any time that you can give to student leaders is a good investment.

In any venue, caution must be used in divulging personal information about persons not present. There are legal as well as biblical principles involved. The general principles are to give sensitive information only to adults who need to know, and only what that person needs to know in order to help.

Cain's question in Genesis 4, "Am I my brother's keeper?" was sarcastic, but the answer is plain. In some sense, you truly are your brother's keeper. As part of that responsibility, you are also his or her discipler. Think of the value of a mother like Susannah Wesley, who patiently spent her life loving and teaching her children. The work of God through her sons, John and Charles, is credited by Christian and secular historians for international revival and for saving England from a bloody revolution such as that which began in France in 1789. Those hands that rocked the cradle of John and Charles Wesley over two hundred years ago truly affected the world.

Whom does God intend for you to train and develop? Of course, you must start with your own home, if you are married or have children. Undoubtedly, though, there are others that God will have you influence through the Christian school.

The most effective administrator is the one who is leading a school filled with faculty and students who are committed to meeting others' needs. This Christlike atmosphere must begin at the top and should be communicated, not through a chain of command, but through a chain of discipleship. Why not evaluate what is happening in your school? Is there a need for a fresh look at your allotment of time? If most of the young people in the Christian school have a desire to please God, and if a few have the boldness to speak out, that few will control the atmosphere. Disciple your staff members so that they may disciple students. In so doing you will help parents to raise up a generation of young people who have a heart for God. Make it your goal to produce graduates who understand biblical discipleship because you have modeled it effectively for them.

References

Goetsch, John and Mark Rasmussen. (n.d.). *Mentoring and modeling.* Lancaster, CA: Revival Books, West Coast Baptist College.

Jameison, Faussett, and Brown. (n.d.). *Commentary Critical and Explanatory on the Whole Bible.* CrossWalk.com. Accessed 21 July 2006. <http://bible.crosswalk.com/Commentaries/JamiesonFaussetBrown/jfb.cgi?book=1th&chapter=2#1Th2_7>

Thayer's and Smith's Bible dictionary. (n.d.). CrossWalk.com. Accessed 24 July 2007. <http://bible1.crosswalk.com/Lexicons/ Greek/grk.cgi?number=3870&version=kjv>

The Wise, the Simple, the Fool and the Scorner

When you need the wisdom of Solomon

Christlikeness, the goal of Christian education, is manifested in students who are wise, discerning, and spiritually mature. Proverbs 1:5 describes such a student: "A wise man will hear, and will increase learning; and a man of understanding shall attain unto wise counsels." This student actually listens to you—and gets the point! More than that, he does what he should do! Wisdom can be defined as the desire and ability to make choices that honor God. How many of your students are progressing toward this kind of wisdom? Wise students are a joy to work with, and it is a privilege to have them in your school.

One of the most neglected areas of Scripture is how to deal with the four types of people: the wise, the simple, the fool, and the scorner. The success of the Christian school depends on applying biblical principles for each of these categories of students. Working with young people requires "the wisdom of Solomon"—and that's exactly what the book of Proverbs provides! The book of

Proverbs becomes the administrator's handbook, teaching how to recognize and respond to different needs. As you apply God's Word consistently in working with students, God will allow you the privilege of working with wise students. [11]

The Wise

Even though there is no perfect young person in your school, you can see the ones whose lives are characterized by the desire to do right. The Bible gives some distinguishing marks.

Characteristics of the wise

- A wise young person desires to live a righteous life.
  - *"A man of understanding walketh uprightly."* (Proverbs 15:21)
- He is eager to learn and, therefore, continually increases in knowledge.
  - *"The heart of him that hath understanding seeketh knowledge."* (15:14)
  - "Wise men lay up knowledge." (10:14)
  - "The heart of the prudent getteth knowledge; and the ear of the wise seeketh knowledge." (18:15)
  - The wise person continues to increase in knowledge and puts that knowledge to good use.
- He is teachable.
  - *"Give instruction to a wise man, and he will be yet wiser: teach a just man, and he will increase in learning."* (9:9)
  - *"The wise in heart will receive commandments."* (10:8)
- He obtains counsel before making important decisions.
  - *"Only by pride cometh contention: but with the well advised is wisdom."* (13:10)

---

11   *Wellsprings of Life,* by Donald Orthner, is a topical categorization of the Proverbs. It is the pattern for this first section, "The Wise," and is the source of the analysis and verse choices for the other sections.

- "Hear counsel, and receive instruction, that thou mayest be wise in thy latter end." (19:20)
- *"He that harkeneth unto counsel is wise."* (12:15)
- He accepts and benefits from correction.
  - *"The ear that heareth the reproof of life abideth among the wise. … He that heareth reproof getteth understanding."* (15:31-32)
  - *"Reprove one that hath understanding, and he will understand knowledge."* (19:25)
  - *"A reproof entereth more into a wise man than an hundred stripes into a fool."* (17:10)

Response to the wise

Having recognized the wise young person demonstrating these qualities, what should be the response of the administrator? The first response is found in Proverbs 21:11—teach him: "When the scorner is punished, the simple is made wise: and when the wise is instructed, he receiveth knowledge." Administration and faculty should teach, disciple, and encourage these young people. Often the word "potential" is used to describe the students who demonstrate natural leadership abilities—with or without the right application of that leadership. That potential is a reality and administrators should develop those young people, but never to the neglect of developing every wise student to the level of his or her own capacity for leadership. The Christian school administrator and faculty ought to disciple the wise young people in the student body.

Not only should your response to the wise students be to teach them, but you should also allow them to teach and influence others. "In the fear of the Lord is strong confidence: and his children shall have a place of refuge" (Proverbs 14:26). When wise young people set the tone of a school, the school becomes a place of refuge; their influence creates an environment in which it is safe for others to do right, free from the mocking of scorners. Consider ways in which you can allow wise young people to exert appropriate leadership in the student body.

Honor the students who want to do right. Class officers may be nominated by the students, but before their names appear on a ballot, they should be screened by a council involving some or all of the teachers, administration, and pastoral staff. Any leadership position, even being on a sports team or musical ministry team, requires a higher level of commitment to doing right. Let these be positions of honor.

The faculty and leadership must support the young people who demonstrate a heart for God.

The Simple

The simple student has not yet assimilated biblical wisdom. This student may have heard it, but has not yet thought it through and applied it to his or her own life.

Characteristics of the simple

- He Lacks wisdom.
    - *"When the scorner is punished, the simple is made wise: and when the wise is instructed, he receiveth knowledge."* (21:11)
- He is easily misled.
    - "The simple believeth every word: but the prudent man looketh well to his going." (14:15)
- He is susceptible to temptation.
    - *"For at the window of my house I looked through my casement, And beheld among the simple ones, I discerned among the youths, a young man void of understanding, Passing through the street near her corner; and he went the way to her house, In the twilight, in the evening, in the black and dark night:*

> *And, behold, there met him a woman with the attire of an*
> *harlot, and subtil of heart."* (7:6-10)

- He unwittingly stumbles into trouble.
  - *"A prudent man foreseeth the evil, and hideth himself: but*
    the simple pass on, and are punished." (22:3)
- He is content in his ignorance.
  - *"How long ye simple ones, will ye love simplicity? And the scorners*
    delight in their scorning, and fools hate knowledge? (1:22)

Christian schools contain many simple young people. They certainly do not see themselves as simple, and on many occasions the parents do not realize it either. The evidence, however, is clear: they are easily misled and get into trouble. Sometimes their parents say that they are "followers" as some degree of excuse. Parents may say or imply that their child's problem is "his [or her] friends" or "the wrong crowd."

Response to the simple

What does God say about the response of the Christian school administrator to the simple ones? The simple will be warned through the example of punished sinners:

> *"When the scorner is punished, the simple is made wise: and*
> *when the wise is instructed, he receiveth knowledge"* (21:11)
> *"Smite a scorner, and the simple will beware: and reprove one that*
> *hath understanding, and he will understand knowledge"* (19:25).

The simple one will learn from the proper, swift handling of the fool and the scorner. There are many simple ones that administrators and teachers could salvage if they would deal with the fool and the scorner in a more biblical way.

Punishment of the simple one, chastening, is also important. When the simple student receives the same punishment as the fool, he or she may decide that the pleasure of sin is not worth the price.

> *"My son, despise not the chastening of the LORD; neither be weary of his correction: For whom the LORD loveth he correcteth; even as a father the son in whom he delighteth. (3:11-12)*

Another response to the simple one is to teach him God's truth while he or she is still able to learn it. That is the major purpose of the Proverbs:

> *"The proverbs of Solomon the son of David, king of Israel ... To give subtilty to the simple, to the young man knowledge and discretion. (1:1, 4)*

The personification of wisdom in Proverbs 8 calls out specifically to the simple:

> *"O ye simple, understand wisdom: and, ye fools, be ye of an understanding heart. Hear; for I will speak of excellent things; and the opening of my lips shall be right things. For my mouth shall speak truth; and wickedness is an abomination to my lips. Receive my instruction, and not silver; and knowledge rather than choice gold. For wisdom is better than rubies; and all the things that may be desired are not to be compared to it." (8:5-7, 10-11)*

The admonition is to consistently discipline (i.e., punish) and to disciple (i.e., teach, lead, provide structure for) the simple one. The discipline of the fool and the scorner also helps the simple become wise. This may appear to be an easy proposition, but there has to be an absolute commitment on the part of the faculty and administrator to follow the commands and the principles of these passages.

The Fool

The fool knows what is right and deliberately chooses to do wrong. Charles Ryrie sums up this kind of person as "one who is morally perverse, not mentally deficient. [He] is described as to his belief ('no God') and behavior ('no good'). His is a practical rather than a theoretical atheist" (note for Psalm 14:1). He acts as if there is no God. Proverbs describes many evidences of the fool.

Characteristics of the fool

* He is self-reliant and proud.
  - "He that trusteth in his own heart is a fool." (28:26)
  - *"The way of a fool is right in his own eyes."* (12:15)
* He lacks wisdom.
  - "Wisdom is too high for a fool: he openeth not his mouth in the gate." (24:7)
  - "A fool hath no delight in understanding, but that his heart may discover itself." (18:2)
* He rejects godly instruction.
  - *"Fools despise wisdom and instruction. ... How long, ye simple ones, will ye love simplicity? And the scorners delight in their scorning, and fools hate knowledge?"* (1:7, 22)
  - A fool might be described this way: "You can't tell him anything; he knows it all."
* He is deceived by his own folly. He does not recognize how foolish he is.
  - "The folly of the fools is deceit." (14:8)
  - "The foolishness of fools is folly." (14:24)
* He enjoys his sin. He thinks it's "cool."
  - "It is as sport to a fool to do mischief." (10:23)
  - "It is abomination to fools to depart from evil." (13:9)
  - "Fools make a mock at [imitate as funny] sin." (14:9)
  - "Folly is joy to him that is destitute of wisdom." (15:21)

- He lacks self-control.
  - *"A fool's wrath is presently known."* (12:16)
  - *"The fool rageth, and is confident."* (14:16)
  - *"A fool layeth open his folly."* (13:16)
- He disdains and grieves his authorities.
  - "He that begetteth a fool doeth it to his sorrow: and the father of a fool hath no joy." (17:21)
  - "A fool despiseth his father's instruction." (15:5)
  - "A foolish man despiseth his mother." (15:20)
  - *"A stone is heavy, and the sand weighty; but a fool's wrath is heavier than them both."* (27:3)

Response to the fool.

The fool must be handled properly if he is to be rescued and if the simple one is to receive instruction. In many Christian schools, the fool and the scorner are being handled in the way that secular psychologists or counselors propose rather than the Bible way. The world's psychology often looks for causes to blame, such as people in the past and problems of life. Sometimes there is more focus on outside influences than on personal responsibility for choices. A Christian counselor should be concerned with the pressures and problems which a young person faces. These are real factors. However, the focus must always be on the choices that the one being counseled has made, and what new choices of obedience to God's Word must be substituted. This power of personal choice, directed by the Word of God and empowered by the Holy Spirit, is the key to change. You must handle the fool and the scorner biblically if you are going to help them and if your school is to going to have a Christ-honoring atmosphere. God will bless consistent obedience to His Word.

The Bible has a clearly established plan. First, the Christian school leader is not to rely on the fool.

*"He that sendeth a message by the hand of a fool cutteth off
the feet, and drinketh damage." (26:6)*

The fool should not be placed in any level of school leadership.
Sometimes authorities give a leadership role to an able but self-
willed young person, hoping that he or she will be encouraged to
do right by that expression of trust. This plan is a mistake. It sends
the wrong message to everybody. Acknowledge and honor each
right step, but let positions of leadership be earned by consistent
patterns of right attitudes and actions.

Second, the faculty and administrator are admonished not to
debate with a fool.

*"If a wise man contendeth with a foolish man, whether he
rage or laugh, there is no rest." (29:9)*

*"Speak not in the ears of a fool for he will despise the wisdom
of thy words." (23:9)*

Often adults are guilty of trying to debate with the young person
in this category because they care. They earnestly desire change for
that student's own good. But it will not work. If he is a fool, he will
despise even the wisest words (23:9). Your intentions may be good,
but the result will be disappointing, even counterproductive. The
best thing you can do for a fool is to explain simply what you must
do and then move on to action, the appropriate punishment.

Remember, however, that you are dealing with children and
young people. Never assume that a student is beyond help. Hope
for and pray for repentance. Sincerely and earnestly work for
change. Love "beareth all things, believeth all things, hopeth all
things, endureth all things" (1 Corinthians 13:7). Further, it can
be difficult, sometimes impossible, to discern between the simple
and the fool. Do not rush to judgment.

Third, the necessary response for a fool, as for simple ones, is punishment.

> *"Judgments are prepared for scorners, and stripes for the back of fools." (19:29)*
> *"A whip for the horse; a bridle for the ass, and a rod for the fool's back." (26:3)*

Ecclesiastes 8:11 adds another element: punishment must not be delayed: "Because sentence against an evil work is not executed speedily, therefore the heart of the sons of men is fully set in them to do evil." Swift and significant response is critical to establishing an appropriate atmosphere in the school. The discipline of the fool will not only help the simple one, but the reaction of the student will also assist the administrator in deciding whether he or she is a scorner. True, "no chastening for the present seemeth to be joyous" (Hebrews 12:11), but scorners actively hate correction (Proverbs 13:1, 15:12). The Christian school must not allow a fool to control the atmosphere or remain long in the school without evidence of progress.

The Scorner

The scorner is a fool who has gone one step further: he or she influences others. Also called a scoffer, this student communicates disdain for the rules and principles of the Christian school. This attitude may be expressed in words or nonverbally, as in facial expression, sighs, or a posture assumed in response to a reproof. Proverbs describes the scorner in the following ways:

Characteristics of the scorner.
- He is filled with pride.
  - "Proud and haughty scorner is his name, who dealeth in proud wrath." (21:24)

- He will not accept correction.
  - "A scorner loveth not one that reproveth him: neither will he go unto the wise." (15:12)
  - "A scorner heareth not rebuke." (13:1)
- He mocks truth.
  - *"And the scorners delight in their scorning, and fools hate knowledge."* (1:22)
- He enjoys being contemptuous.
  - "An ungodly witness scorneth judgment and the mouth of the wicked devoureth iniquity." (19:28)
- He causes problems for others.
  - *"Scornful men bring a city into a snare."* (29:8)

Response to the scorner

The necessary response to the scorner is described in the following ways:

- Do not attempt to reprove or counsel him.
  - *"He that reproveth a scorner getteth to himself shame: and he that rebuketh a wicked man getteth himself a blot. Reprove not a scorner, lest he hate thee."* (9:7-8)
  - The reproofs should have been coming long before this point. Of course a student must know what he has done wrong and why it is wrong. That should be very familiar information to the student by the time you conclude that he is a scorner. The admonition not to reprove a scorner means that, when the time of expulsion comes, there is no point in debating those matters. A paper trail is very important. Keep a record of telephone calls, emails, and notes to parents. If you have not been consistent in keeping in touch with the parents, you are at fault.

- He must be cast out.
  - *"Cast out the scorner, and contention shall go out; yea, strife and reproach shall cease."* (22:10)
- His punishment will warn the simple ones.
  - *"When the scorner is punished, the simple is made wise: and when the wise is instructed, he receiveth knowledge."* (21:11)
  - *"Smite a scorner, and the simple will beware: and reprove one that hath understanding, and he will understand knowledge."* (19:25)

The administrator must act. In many schools the administrator and faculty spend an inordinate amount of their time providing counsel and instruction to the fool and scorner. Granted, it is important to establish the facts with certainty before a young person is disciplined. It is a terrible thing to unjustly punish or to prematurely expel a student who could have been helped. However, once the facts are established and if the student's direction is a clearly consistent pattern, the administrator must take biblically appropriate action. The schools that are most effective in developing Christlike character do not allow a scorner to remain in the school because that kind of student can control the spiritual atmosphere. The scorner will stand out and should be dealt with swiftly by the administrator. It is not because there is a lack of love on the part of the administrator but because there is simple obedience to God and desire to protect the other students.

In reality, the scorner chooses his fate. If you pick up one end of a stick, you get the other; you can choose your actions but you cannot choose their consequences. As the administrator and faculty provide consistent discipline, the young person will have to decide whether he or she wants to stay in the Christian school enough to change.

"Are these lines written because we intend to 'write off' this person and refuse to try to help him?" asks Gordon Dickson

(2005). And he answers with a strong "no." Dickson cites God's pattern in dealing with Israel. When Israel rebelled, God gave them over to the power of their enemies. When their hearts were softened, He redeemed them (p. 39). Christian school leaders should hurt for these students and their families, but the only way to help the scorner is to let him or her reap the consequence of his or her actions.

No expulsion has to be forever. Whether it is the student who uncharacteristically committed a major violation, or whether it is the scorner who gradually built up evidence against himself or herself, there should be a plan for restoration in response to genuine repentance. "Developing a Spiritual Restoration Program" (Burrell, 1998) develops several ideas. Notable among them are these:

- The desire for restoration must be student initiated. Restoration is not something the school pushes the student into.
- The student must be genuinely repentant. Repentance is not something the parents can push the student into. When students just go through the motions, when they do a ritualistic set of things just to get back into the school, there is great danger for the other students in the school.
- There must be safeguards set in place for the future, including local church involvement.
- The student must make request to a governing body, such as a school board or the school committee of the deacons of a church-run school. This step provides safety for the administrator.
- The student must ask forgiveness of those hurt and make restoration; some loss must be restored. If a sin is widely known, speaking to the student body allows the offender to acknowledge the offence and to put it in the past.

- The student must be mentored by an administrator or faculty member.
- There still must be significant consequences.

The administrator must be tough and tender. Administrative leadership in the Christian school is not for cowards. Often the emotion that accompanies difficult decisions is intense. Often parents do not understand. You must "be strong in the Lord and in the power of his might" (Ephesians 6:10). You must rest confidently in the truths of the Word of God. You are admonished to speak the truth in love, even when the truth is hard to speak (Ephesians 4:15). Any confrontation with a fool or scorner must be handled in the spirit of love, care, and concern—but it must be biblically handled. If there is a young person in the Christian school who has no evident desire for the Lord, has shown evidence of being a fool or scorner, and is leading a group of simple ones in the wrong way, the faculty and the administrator have a responsibility to challenge that student. He must not be allowed to promote an ungodly lifestyle or atmosphere within the student body.

A balance of opposites is given in Proverbs 22:10-11: "Cast out the scorner, and contention shall go out; yea, strife and reproach shall cease. He that loveth pureness of heart, for the grace of his lips the king shall be his friend." Casting out the scorner brings an end to contention: bad relations between school leadership and students, or between students who are doing right and the fools and scorners. Reproach, the bad testimony caused by rebellious students, will cease. The balancing effect is that the administrator becomes a friend and encourager of the young people who love pureness of heart, who want to do right.

You must work with some students, attempting to recover them from Satan's snare (2 Timothy 2:26). But do not neglect the other young people who are going the right direction. Do not let discipline problems eclipse your positive discipleship ministry. Working with the young people who desire to please God will be worth the effort. Encourage them to be strong in their convictions.

God will bless your efforts as you deal biblically with the wise, the simple, the fool, and the scorner.

References

Burrell, D. (1998). Developing a spiritual restoration program. *Journal for Christian Educators.* 4 (4), 10-13.

Dickson, G. (2005, September-October). What about the scorner? *FrontLine,* p. 39.

Orthner, D. (1989). *Wellsprings of life: Understanding Proverbs.* Greenville, SC: Adon books.

Ryrie, C. C. (1978). Note at Psalm 14:1. *Ryrie study Bible.* Chicago: Moody Bible Institute.

Discipleship Through Discipline

From the external to the internal
From the internal to the eternal [12]

The students are all in their seats—early! Even before the last tones of the starting bell have died away, pencils are poised and an expectant hush pervades the classroom. Not your classroom? Well, I've never seen it either, but it's a nice dream. If teaching were just the communication of academic content to eager minds ... well, where would be the character training? Discipline, that is, *developing the disciplines of life*, is a major part of developing Christlike character in students.

Discipline is a small part of a larger picture. Classroom management is the structure and conduct of all elements of the learning environment. Discipline, in this paradigm, is the part of classroom management that focuses on directing and correcting student behavior.

12   The authors express their appreciation to Theodore Caucutt for several ideas in this chapter which were derived from his article published in the *Journal for Christian Educators*. *Dr. Richard Harris contributed significantly to the development of practices relating to biblical character formation and to the concept of training "Champions for Christ."*

Even in their college years, many education majors indicate classroom management, discipline in particular, as their major concern. Fear is unnecessary, but awareness of the importance of this area is appropriate. Discipline is essential to every teacher's success and to the success of the schools in which they serve. Teachers with a good grasp of this skill are essential to the mission of the Christian school. The administrator, faculty, and staff must effectively manage the school's disciplinary process if the school is to accomplish the development of Christlike character. Even though discipline is vital to the success of the Christian school, a successful disciplinary program is not complex. The challenge of developing young people with self-control should inspire hope and confidence, not dread.

Major Styles of School Management

There are infinite variations of management styles, but most schools fit into one of the following three categories.

The *authoritarian* style of management is very strong in structure and discipline but is weaker in the manifestation of love, care, and concern. Authoritarian schools may have a punitive feel in the classroom. They typically produce students who outwardly conform to rules but have little internalization of principles. Students obey the school's rules, but those rules are not their own convictions or philosophy. Because these students do not have their own strong convictions, they are sometimes blown off course by the first new ideas they meet after leaving such a school. Other students maintain a quiet rebellion. While in school, they do what they have to do, but their rejection of the school's standards becomes apparent immediately after graduation. The faculty and staff in these schools focus on the outward appearance and action, but little is accomplished in the heart.

The *permissive* style of management is strong in the manifestation of love and concern but is very weak in structure and discipline. The words *grace* and *love* are used often in these schools while ignoring *righteousness* and *holiness* in Christian living. The testimony of these schools is very weak. They typically do not produce a Christlike product. Scorners often control the atmosphere, and Christlike attitudes are stifled among the students.

The *authoritative* style of management is strong in structure and discipline and is equally strong in love and nurturing. The concern for the spiritual growth of offending students is not just an attitude held by teachers and administration; it is an observable reality manifested in word and deed. Biblical love will not tolerate wrong actions and bad attitudes. However, problems are met with disciple-making discipline, rather than mere punishment. It is marked by "speaking the truth in love" (Ephesians 4:15). Like the Lord Jesus, it is balanced, "full of [both] grace and truth" (John 1:14). Authoritative management is the biblical model.

A concern for truth leads to strong convictions. An appreciation of grace leads to compassion. These qualities, and the results of their balance or imbalance can be expressed as a formula:

Conviction without compassion = contention.
Compassion without conviction = compromise.
Compassion with conviction = Christlikeness.

Every standard of conduct set up by the Christian school should have a biblical basis. Though there may not be an explicit command in Scripture for every standard of behavior, the school administrator should be able to justify each standard as an application of a biblical principle. For instance, getting homework done on time reflects the principles of Romans 12:11, "Not slothful in business; fervent in spirit; serving the Lord." Respect for authorities is based on Romans 13:7, "Render therefore to all their dues: ... honour to whom honour." Students should be taught the biblical principles as well as the standard of behavior so that they can learn to live by principles, not just by rules.

Every student and staff member is a sinner, even if most or all are saved by grace. As recipients of grace, school leaders should understand the need to deal with others as God has dealt with them. The demeanor of the staff must always demonstrate God's love. Authoritative leadership recognizes both the need for correction and the need for grace.

The Bible has much to say on this balance of grace and truth, which is characteristic of authoritative leadership. Consider these biblical ideas:

Warning is required.

"For I have told [Eli] that I will judge his house for ever for the iniquity which he knoweth; because his sons made themselves vile, and he restrained them not." (1 Samuel 3:13)

Obedience is the norm in many relationships.

"Children, obey your parents in the Lord: for this is right. ... Servants, be obedient to them that are your masters according to the flesh, with fear and trembling, in singleness of your heart, as unto Christ; ... With good will doing service, as to the Lord, and not to men: Knowing that whatsoever good thing any man doeth, the same shall he receive of the Lord, whether he be bond or free. And, ye masters, do the same things unto them, forbearing threatening: knowing that your Master also is in heaven; neither is there respect of persons with him." (Ephesians 6:1,5, 7-9)

Let every soul be subject unto the higher powers. For there is no power but of God: the powers that be are ordained of God. Whosoever therefore resisteth the power, resisteth the ordinance of God: and they that resist shall receive to themselves damnation. (Romans 13:1-2)

Wrong discipline can destroy, right discipline protects.

> *"Fathers, provoke not your children to anger, lest they be discouraged."* (Colossians 3:21)
>
> *"But we were gentle among you, even as a nurse cherisheth her children."* (1 Thessalonians 2:7)

Words have weight.

> *"Let your speech be alway with grace, seasoned with salt, that ye may know how ye ought to answer every man."* (Colossians 4:6)

Those who administer discipline will give account.

Along with the warning to "masters" above (Ephesians 6:9), consider these:

> *"My brethren, be not many masters, knowing that we shall receive the greater condemnation. For in many things we offend all. If any man offend not in word, the same is a perfect man, and able also to bridle the whole body."* (James 3:1-2)
>
> *"Whoso shall offend one of these little ones which believe in me, it were better for him that a millstone were hanged about his neck, and that he were drowned in the depth of the sea."* (Matthew 18:6)
>
> *"But Jesus said, Suffer little children, and forbid them not, to come unto me; for of such is the kingdom of heaven."* (Matthew 19:14)

Biblical discipline is not complex, but it takes balance and courage. It takes a tough and tender Christian leader.

The Reason for Discipline

In a war, having the right allies is important to victory. In the battle for the souls of children and teens, their parents are the most important of earthly allies. To have them on your side from the start, you must start with your philosophy of discipline clearly presented. Teach both the underlying purpose of the whole disciplinary system and the reasons for the particular rules. Deal with the big picture and the details.

A clearly articulated, thoroughly biblical system of discipline can help the home as well as the school. The Christian school, as an extension of the home, should support and reinforce the process that parents have in place at home. Yet, many parents have not thought through a biblically sound discipline system for their own homes. This difference is not necessarily opposition to your standards; it may be the lack of an articulated plan in the minds of the parents. In this, the administrator humbly takes the role of discipling the parents too. If the behavior problems of a second-grade child require a conference with the administrator, God is giving the administrator a discipleship opportunity. If the child is being disobedient at school the first question to ask the parents is, "Does he (or she) obey at home?" In today's culture the answer is likely to be, "Oh, yes, that is why I cannot understand why he (or she) is causing such a problem for this teacher. The teacher must not be approaching things properly. Maybe you should provide some extra instruction for that teacher." A follow-up question by a wise administrator would be, "Please tell me exactly what you mean when you say that Johnny is very obedient at home." This gets to the parents' concept of what obedience is. A discussion on the definition of obedience may reveal a large portion of the problem.

The following definition of obedience can work well for all parents and should be used in the Christian school:

> Obedience: Doing exactly what you are told to do, doing it immediately, and doing it with the right heart attitude.

If a child violates any aspect of this three-part definition, he or she is not being completely obedient and needs correction.

A second word that often needs discussion is *consistency*. While no one can be 100% consistent, Christian leaders must strive for this in their own lives, in their homes and in their Christian schools. If the teacher is striving to be consistent and the child is not accustomed to observing this in the home, this situation may present another opportunity to disciple the parents. The Christian school faculty must consistently enforce the standards and expectations of the school. The wise teacher or administrator will help everyone—child, teacher, and parents—by helping the parents to understand the value of approaching obedience and correction in a consistent manner.

Consistency may be described in the following way:

No differences ...

> Between what you say and do
> From one day to the next
> Between dad and mom
> Between the parents and any other authority in the child's life, such as the Christian school teacher

When the parents approach the behavior of the child in the same, consistent way that the Christian school is attempting to follow, the opportunity to successfully assist the parents is immeasurably increased.

Four basic truths must be accepted by both the home and the school to successfully partner in a discipline and discipleship program. Disagreement on these important points will result in constant battles.

The Nature of Man Is Sinful, Selfish, and Rebellious.

"Foolishness is bound in the heart of a child; but the rod of correction shall drive it far from him." (Proverbs 22:15)

> *"The heart is deceitful above all things, and desperately wicked: who can know it?"* (Jeremiah 17:9)

Children may often be sweet and kind, but they are not naturally good. All of people have within them the tendency toward wrongdoing, even though it will be manifested differently in different people. God gave the Law, in part, to show how far short of God's standard of holiness even the best people fall (Galatians 3:21-24; 1 Timothy 1:8-9).

The Fallen Nature of Man Requires Restraint.

> *"For I know that in me (that is, in my flesh,) dwelleth no good thing for to will is present with me; but how to perform that which is good I find not. For the good that I would I do not: but the evil which I would not, that I do. Now if I do that I would not, it is no more I that do it, but sin that dwelleth in me. I find then a law, that, when I would do good, evil is present with me. For I delight in the law of God after the inward man: But I see another law in my members."* (Romans 7:18-23)

God has given the Bible and human authority (Romans 13) to restrain man because the nature of man is sinful. In any governmental system, a self-disciplined citizenry will be a blessing to those in authority. The judicial system is designed to restrain the undisciplined. Even the best Christian school, having leadership, faculty, and a student body focused on operating biblically, will still have the flesh with which to contend. A wise administrator and faculty will recognize the need for a structured, consistent disciplinary program designed to restrain man's fallen nature.

The school must steadfastly maintain high standards of dress and conduct. This position is not popular with some, but whom do you most want to please: vociferous and worldly students and parents, or the ones who value high standards? If a school is going to help develop Christlike students, school leaders must not allow the works of the flesh to be in control of the atmosphere through the carnal students. Strong standards of dress (Romans 12:1-2; Galatians 5:16-25), behavioral expectations (Romans 12:1), and music (Colossians 3:16; Psalm 40:3), must be maintained. The Bible clearly states that "the flesh lusteth against the spirit, and the spirit against the flesh: and these are contrary the one to the other: so that ye cannot do the things that ye would" (Galatians 5:17). Expect resistance. The standards and expectations of the school must be strong.

Parents—and school authorities—must understand the difference between moral standards and institutional standards. Some things are always right or wrong. A rule about honesty or respect is a *moral standard*. By contrast, *institutional standards* are the practical applications of principles. They may be the attempt to define modesty by creation of a dress code (*application* of a moral principle) or they may just be matters of practical functionality: designated parking areas for students, for example.

Corporate standards are a fair analogy to the rules of the Christian school. Major companies like IBM have their dress codes because they believe those standards help to accomplish their goals. These are institutional standards, not moral standards. If people can submit to those standards to work at IBM, people should be able to submit to sometimes-debatable rules, realizing that the school must draw a line somewhere.

Keep a balance. You cannot judge a person's spirituality by standards of conduct. For example, boys should not have "long hair." But how long is long? A student's father may be a godly man whose hair would not fit the dress code of the school. That is not a problem. But parent and child must realize that, once they agree for the child to abide by a dress code in order to attend the school, their willing, respectful submission to those standards for the son becomes a moral issue. It is a matter of respecting God-ordained authorities.

Yet, for a family to benefit from the Christian school, the family's standards cannot be vastly different from the school's standards. That discussion is part of the new-family interview. If a family is very different in their standards, the interviewer should help them weigh carefully whether they can accept the school's standards.

Parents must understand that institutional standards are not always moral standards, but there must be some consistent way to define boundaries if there are to be boundaries at all. While no two people are going to draw their boundaries exactly the same way, there must be basic agreement about the necessity of *having* biblical boundaries. The Bible is clear in its teachings: there are rights and wrongs in the standards of dress, in the behavior that is expected of believers, and in music. The goal of defining standards should be to stay as far away from the flesh and the world as possible. If Biblical character formation is the priority, serious consideration must be given to maintaining standards.

A Disciplinary Program Establishes Order and Accountability.

The Old Testament law was implemented also to establish order and accountability by external control. In the New Testament, the Apostle Paul advocates obedience even to a pagan, secular government:

> *Let every soul be subject unto the higher powers. For there is no power but of God: the powers that be are ordained of God. Whosoever therefore resisteth the power, resisteth the ordinance of God: and they that resist shall receive to themselves damnation. For rulers are not a terror to good works, but to the evil. Wilt thou then not be afraid of the*

power? Do that which is good, and thou shalt have praise of
the same: For he is the minister of God to thee for good. But
if thou do that which is evil, be afraid, for he beareth not the
sword in vain: for he is the minister of God, a revenger to
execute wrath upon him that doeth evil. (Romans 13:1-4)

Students must learn submission to authority. All rebellion
against authority is ultimately rebellion against God, who ordained
those authorities. It is important for Christian school leadership
to establish appropriate regulations, guidelines, and procedures
in order to establish an orderly institution. As violations occur,
constant enforcement must be in place to maintain order.

Consistency is critical. Students should *expect* disciplinary
measures when they violate the rules. They should not be wondering
whether the school authorities will do anything "this time."

You will not always get it right. Christian school leaders
should admit when they have made mistakes. On the other hand,
students cannot predicate their obedience on the perfection of
their parents and teachers. One of the most important lessons of
life is learning to submit to imperfect human authority. You must
still lead, and students must still follow. Be humble. Be strong.
Do God's work and lead. You may make mistakes, but the worst
mistake is to do nothing.

Effective Christian school leadership requires a good discipline
structure. The school with an ineffective or inconsistent disciplinary
structure is not just a bad refection on its leadership; it presents a poor
reflection of God as the God of order (1 Corinthians 14:33, 40).

A Disciplinary Program Can Help Develop Self-control.

The goal is self-control. However, a first step toward that
goal is the unpleasant revelation of existing weaknesses. A strong,
consistent disciplinary program will reveal students' weaknesses.

These may sometimes be a revelation to the parents and even to the student. Be aware of that possibility when you are counseling. Parents may come in upset at the school for *causing* a problem in the child's life, when the disciplinary situation has merely *revealed* the problem that was lying dormant all the time.

The revelation of weakness parallels another purpose of the Old Testament law: to reveal all people's need for Christ.

> *Is the law then against the promises of God? God forbid: for if there had been a law given which could have given life, verily righteousness should have been by the law. But the scripture hath concluded all under sin, that the promise by faith of Jesus Christ might be given to them that believe. But before faith came, we were kept under the law, shut up unto the faith which should afterwards be revealed. Wherefore the law was our schoolmaster to bring us unto Christ, that we might be justified by faith.* (Galatians 3:21-24.)

The fact that young people are likely to break a rule is no reason to avoid having the rule. The law, established by God, reveals that all "come short of the glory of God" (Romans 3:23). Likewise, the disciplinary system in a school will reveal weaknesses in the lives of the young people. As the weaknesses, or sins, are revealed, a wise teacher or administrator must work in concert with the parents to: (a) restrain the student in his weak areas (b) remind him of God's view of sin and of His love, and (c) review the biblical steps necessary to gain victory over this area in his life. A broken rule indicates a need for discipleship as well as punishment.

God wants young people to possess self-control. The word *temperance* is used for this quality in 2 Peter chapter 1 ("Giving all diligence, add to your faith ... temperance," vv. 5 & 6) and in the fruit of the Spirit passage, Galatians 5:22-23. Self-control can be developed through the application of external control. Consider Hebrews 12:11: "Now no chastening for the present seemeth to be joyous, but grievous: nevertheless afterward it yieldeth the peaceable fruit of righteousness unto them which are exercised thereby." This passage speaks of both God's training His children and of parents training their own children. The brief time that young people are in their parents' homes or in Christian schools is a brief, sacred, and solemn opportunity to help them develop self-control. Character development is not an option: it is integral to Christian education.

Rules alone will not produce godly young people. They reveal the weaknesses. Granted, rules protect and direct; but assuming that a rule can correct problem behavior or attitudes is similar to assuming that a thermometer can cure an illness. The thermometer reveals that there is a problem; correct application of medicine and prayer will cure the illness. A biblical disciplinary structure will provide an opportunity to restrain man's fallen nature, to establish order and accountability, and to reveal the weaknesses present. A wise faculty and staff will allow the Lord to use them to disciple the students. God will work through His Word to produce lasting change in the lives of Christian young people.

Discipline as Discipleship

The basic three elements of discipline are *communication, control,* and *correction*. Not coincidentally, these are similar to the ways in which the Word of God is profitable: "for doctrine, for reproof, for correction, for instruction in righteousness" (2 Timothy 3:16-17). The three elements of discipline, if implemented effectively and consistently, will aid the Christian school staff in producing an educational atmosphere that will please the Lord.

Communication

Good communication begins with the enrollment interview. The school's philosophy, the administrator's sincere concern, and some of the specific rules should be part of that first meeting. Among rules worthy of early communication are those likely to bring questions, such as a ban on certain kinds of music or on going to movie theaters. Above all, communicate the reasons for the rules, and communicate everything in a spirit of loving concern. You want parents to see that you are not just *against* evil movies and rock music: you are *for* developing purity and Christlike character.

The communication must be clearly established in a parent/student handbook. That book becomes the point of reference, and parents will hold the school to what is written in it. Therefore, it must be current and flexible. Flexibility for meeting unforeseen challenges can be built in by such phrases as "The administration reserves the right to establish new policies as needed. Any new policies will be communicated to parents and students." Another base to cover is the "letter of the law" clause:

> Some rules exist just to provide order, and others involve setting a clear and enforceable standard in issues of right and wrong. All of the rules have one goal: developing Christlikeness. If a student obeys the letter of the law but is not in keeping with the spirit of the law, that situation will require conference and change.

Keep the handbook current. If there is a rule you no longer consider important, announce that fact and change it in the next printing. Do not have rules that you do not enforce.

Every year should begin with a parent orientation. This meeting is one of the most important of the year for keeping your school families on board with your philosophy. Make it special. Make it fun. And make it count! Parents and students must know or be reminded of a few rules that they may not naturally think of, from parking places to dress code. (Dress code should also be communicated in a letter early in the summer, before parents have bought the year's wardrobe.) Parents also want practical things like locating lockers and classrooms. They want to meet their children's teachers. Make the evening meet the parents' needs and expectations, but do not neglect to communicate the philosophy and the practical details of key rules.

Communicating the details of regulations to the parents and students is of great importance, but so is communicating the heart of loving concern. You are not reading them the rule book (and you are not reading them the Riot Acts). You are just helping them to get off to a smooth start. Students and parents should not get a sense that any staff person is against them. They should understand that you love them and want what is best for them.

Some people are quick to condemn as "legalistic" any school with standards of conduct stricter than their own. And sometimes they are right. Two schools may have the same rules—and be equally consistent in enforcing them—and one school is legalistic, and the other one is not. The difference is attitude. This discussion ignores the salvation-by-works legalism of Galatians. The sort of legalism which occurs in schools usually is the attitude that doing certain things makes one a better Christian. Your students are not better Christians because of doing better things. This cause-effect sequence is reversed. When people do better things because of a desire to please God, that is godly obedience. Being causes doing, not vice versa. Yet, your students still must do right, whether or not they have reached the level of spiritual maturity where they do it for the right reasons. It is the families of these less spiritually mature students who are inclined to call you legalistic. Do not condemn and reject them—such judgment is the legalistic response! Genuinely love them and keep on instructing.

Humility is the oil that smoothes the friction caused by peoples' reactions to rules. (Note: this friction is not caused by the rules themselves.) Some things are clearly right and wrong. In many other areas, a line must be drawn among the shades of gray. Dress, hair, and entertainment are classic areas where good people may draw their personal lines in different places. As a school leader you should humbly admit that the school's way is not the only right way to do everything, even as you firmly retain the responsibility to establish some kind of standard.

Control

Even as the communication to the students and parents continues, the control aspect of the process begins. Three elements promote effective control in a Christian school.

Right environment

Sometimes the school can make it easier to do right. This is the broader "classroom management" side of discipline. A school will have fewer discipline problems if it reduces some of the unnecessary irritants. Have you noticed that it is easier for you to say unkind things when you are tired and hungry? Children are more susceptible to these things than adults. Pay attention to the temperature of the classroom, class size, lighting, playground dynamics, lunchroom policies, methods of transporting students from one point to another. All of these things, and many others, will have an impact on attitudes and behavior. Leadership must give careful consideration to such items. The environment in the Christian school should be conducive to spiritual development, academic training, and appropriate social interaction. Students cannot be allowed to blame their environment for their sin, but the school authorities should do what they can to make it easier to do right.

Go out of your way to be friendly toward students who have spiritual needs and attitude problems. Have a genuinely warm greeting for them in the halls. In so doing, you are building bridges to their souls so that you can reach out to them when the opportunity comes.

Right actions

In the communication stage of the disciplinary process, consequences for violations are made clear. Once a violation occurs the school personnel must simply and lovingly follow through on the prescribed corrective measures.

First, the teacher or administrator should be certain that all of the facts have been established. Even if time is required to check into the situation, establishment of the facts is imperative.

Deal with observable evidence. You are asking for trouble if you expel a student because he or she "has a bad attitude." The student may have the attitude of the scorner and, therefore, must be cast out (Proverbs 22:10), but take the time to do two things. First, attempt to rescue the student. If, however, the student will not change, you must have documented (1) the specific, observable things that manifested the scorner's attitude and (2) all that you have done to try to help the student, including abundant, early communication with the parents.

All discipline should be administered fairly and consistently. Certain violations will receive automatic and pre-determined results. Your handbook may state, for instance, that alcohol, immorality, or drugs require expulsion on the first offense. Other offenses may require additional thought, discernment, and consideration. The key is to constantly follow through on the thoughtfully and prayerfully prepared consequences and to be consistent from one case to the next.

All offenses should be recorded. If a student never does anything major, but is often committing minor infractions, that student needs help. The student who slips and talks in class once is not in the same situation as the student who regularly does the same thing. An angry parent may charge that someone is just picking on his or her child. A list of offenses, dealt with by several different staff members over a long period of time, may help to defuse that anger.

That list should also show that the school communicated with the parents about those problems—with the dates of those notes, emails or phone calls. The parents are God's primary agents in the lives of their children. The Christian school must work with the parents in the training process. The communication lines must be kept open if effective training is to take place.

Right spirit

Be kind and firm. The staff of the Christian school must "speak the truth in love" (Ephesians 4:15). Discipline must be firm and resolute, but love must be ever present in dealings with the students and parents alike. Effective communication of love will cover a multitude of transgressions and misunderstandings.

Be controlled by the Holy Spirit (Galatians 5:22-25). Do you approach a discipline situation with fear, anger, or tension? Those emotions do not mix well with "love, joy, peace, [and] longsuffering." The students will feel as if your anger is directed toward them, as if they are the enemies. That makes it hard to win their souls. Rest in the Lord and rejoice in hope, even as you work through problems. Your mature, godly attitude will go a long way toward building a relationship of love and trust as you seek to help young people and their parents.

Be balanced. This manifestation of love, joy, and peace should not look like giddiness or lack of seriousness. You realize the seriousness of the situation, even as you are trusting in the power of God to bring good results. One mark of maturity in the Christian leader is the capacity to be serious and positive at the same time.

Correction

Discipline is a word with layers of interrelated meanings. Discipline, as punishment unto restoration, has its necessary role. The Bible word is *chastisement* (Hebrews 12). However this discipline is only one part of correction. The larger elements of self-discipline and the disciplines of life are also part of the school's disciplinary focus.

The final stage in the correction process is to provide biblical counsel. This is discipleship. The Word of God is given not only for doctrine and reproof. It also provides correction (shows how to get things right) and instruction in righteousness (how to grow in Christ). The school staff must view their role as more than simply handing out punishments. The demerits, detentions, or tallies are simply tools used to maintain accountability in the student's life. The correction process should include biblical counsel, and at times, restitution.

The faculty and administration are not doing their job unless they are discipling. Not every disciplinary event can become a counseling appointment, but teachers, on the front lines of discipline, must look for opportunities to speak a word of correction as well as of reproof. An appropriate word after class will be long remembered. The administrator must be a master of discipleship, counseling from the Word of God. Sometimes this is just a word in private, or alone in the hallway after school. Sometimes, however, it is an on-going series of sessions complete, with counseling projects and parental involvement.

Direction

The focus of discipline must be discipleship. Discipleship implies relationships. A discipleship focus is people-related and is interested in spiritual development. This is a very time-consuming process, but it is one that will provide eternal rewards. As the students catch the enthusiasm of an active, adventurous walk with God, it becomes exciting to disciple each of them unto Christlikeness. The goal is for each to become a servant who desires to please Christ in every decision that is made and every direction that is taken. This is the only satisfying and fulfilling life. It is encouraging and rewarding to observe this type of progress in a Christian school.

Biblical character formation is a challenging task. It takes the wisdom that can only be provided by God's word and the presence and indwelling of the Holy Spirit. It is a battle fought with the weapons of the armor of God, especially with the Word and prayer. The Scripture says, "For we wrestle not against flesh and blood, but against principalities, against powers, against the rulers of the darkness of this world, against spiritual wickedness in high places" (Ephesians 6:12). Administrators and teachers must recognize where the battle lines are drawn, and must allow the Holy Spirit to use them as they invest their lives in the lives of young people.

Disciplinary Systems

Universal Truths

Christian schools use a variety of disciplinary systems. Most common today are the merit/demerit system, the detention system, Lee Canter's Assertive Discipline system, and the tally system. Administrators and teachers can become very passionate in defense of a particular disciplinary system. The key to the success of the disciplinary structure of a school is found not so much in the system used as in the consistency of using the system.

Never should a student or parent be able to accurately accuse the staff of the school as being inconsistent. If the Word of God and the school handbook state something, the school must consistently enforce it. Leaders must consistently apply God's Word to their own lives and to each decision that is made in the school. As the school staff is discipling the young people, there is nothing more effective in biblical character formation than for a student to emulate a disciple-making teacher or administrator who is walking consistently like Christ.

Yes, every human system will have its own strengths and weaknesses. It is, perhaps, good that administrators and teachers cannot rely on any *system*. They must remain daily and directly dependent on God's power to effect change in their students. There are, however, broad principles present in any good system. Consider God's summation of how to change a life: "By mercy and truth iniquity is purged: and by the fear of the Lord men depart from evil" (Proverbs 16:6).

- *Mercy*—reaching out to one who does not deserve it, meeting repentance with restoration
- *Truth*—unbending standards based in the principles of God's Word
- *Fear of the Lord*—the inward motivation to please God.

There are many good discipline systems, but all of them work toward mercy, truth, and the fear of the Lord. Six qualities are common among good disciplinary systems:

1. Clear and consistent communication with students and parents
2. An ability to remove the students who should not be in the school
3. Recognition of significant progress made by the student
4. Active involvement in the discipleship of students by teachers and the administration
5. Restitution to affected parties
6. A foundation of love and concern for the students

Particular Suggestions

Most of the guidelines for handling discipline outlined here are taken from Dr. Ardell Jacquot's book *Guide to Successful Christian*

Teaching (pp. 58-63). This book has a chapter on "Classroom Control/Discipline," and the whole book is one of the basic resources every Christian teacher and administrator should have.

Keep the rules simple.

The student will be disciplined if he . . .

- Communicates in class without permission
- Gets out of his seat without permission
- Disturbs or violates another student
- Is disobedient to or disrespectful of the teacher

Deal with minor infractions.

- Look at the student
- Talk more softly than usual
- Capitalize on body language
- Shake the head
- Move toward the student
- Be silent and stare
- Ask the student a question

Deal with offenses that need minor punishment

- Call the student's name
- Walk back to the student
- Have the student write sentences (If this is used, the teacher should require the student to copy something neatly from a book.)
- Reprimand verbally
- Ask to see him after class
- Change the student's seat assignment
- Deprive the student of privileges
- Isolate the student from others

Deal with offences that require more severe punishment

- Hold a teacher/student or teacher/parent conference
- Communicate with parents by note or phone call

- Lower the conduct grade
- Arrange a supervisor/student conference
- Utilize the disciplinary system in place
- Send the student to the principal and send a letter home.
- Place the student on behavioral probation
- Use suspension or expulsion as a last resort (Suspension should be isolation in school, not a day to watch TV at home.)

Some things should not be used for correction. Never deliberately embarrass a student. Humiliation shifts the student's focus from what he or she did wrong to the wrong of your action in causing public humiliation. It also alienates the parents who should be your allies. Never use the Bible for punishment. Yes, counsel from the Word. You may require verse memory as part of a series of counseling meetings. You might have the student analyze his or her own actions using Scripture. But do not have students write verses "for punishment."

And never give up hope. Not every chapter has a happy ending, but God keeps on working. "He which hath begun a good work in you will perform it until the day of Jesus Christ" (Philippians 1:6). It may take years of working with a student to see him change. Sometimes the work extends beyond your school. God is not finished with your students when they leave your school, even the lackluster graduates—good enough to get by, but not on fire for God—or the students you have to expel. Be faithful, and you may get some of those precious letters from former students testifying of God's work in their lives and how your loving correction played a part in it.

Although the good disciplinarian is not necessarily a good teacher, every good teacher is a good disciplinarian. In order for a teacher to be effective, he or she must be able to control the class. Likewise, in order for the Christian school to be effective in developing Christlike character, a good disciplinary system must be effectively used.

Every Christian school leader must recognize that his or her leadership represents something about God to the young people (Romans 13:1-4). The attitude and approach to discipline must consistently represent the grace and truth of the Lord as they desire to please God in the process of discipline in the Christian school.

Reference

Caucutt, T. (1985). Developing parental confidence. *Journal for Christian Educators (3)*5, 11.

Jacquot, A. (1984). *Guide to successful Christian teaching*. Chattanooga: American Association of Christian Schools.

Working with Parents

The allied high command [13]

The teachers are afraid of the parents; the parents are afraid of the administrator; and the kids aren't afraid of anyone! Has something gone awry? In God's plan, parents, teachers, and administrators are allies. "We are laborers together with God" (1 Corinthians 3:9). This phrase is rich upon analysis:

1. People certainly are not laborers *with God* in any sense of being equal partners. The Greek expresses God's using His people in His work. Teachers, administrators, and parents are laborers *belonging to God*, fulfilling His command to teach students all things which Christ has commanded. (Matthew 28:20)

2. People also labor *with each other*. They are cooperating in the very real, often very enjoyable, but also very serious business of training the young people in their care. (Galatians 4:1-2)

In this second sense, as the most significant earthly authorities in a student's life, the parents, teachers, and school administrators make up a set of allies, mutually committed to the goal of developing

13   The authors express their appreciation to Theodore Caucutt for several ideas in this chapter which were derived from his article published in the *Journal for Christian Educators.*

Christlikeness in young people. For the children's good, parents, teachers, and administrators are the "allied high command."

However, they all must understand the authority-service structure. The school exists to serve the parents. Granted, the parents have agreed to a certain set of standards and procedures in order to enroll their children in the Christian school. This is not to say, however, that the school is dictating how the parents run their homes. In reality, the parents who entrust their children to the care of a given Christian school should already be committed to the general directions of the school. Even though no two homes will have exactly the same set of goals and standards, the parents who have partnered with your school are there because they believe that your school will help them achieve their own goals for their children's lives. If they have to go along with some standard that is not precisely what they would have established, to these parents that adjustment is a small thing compared to the value of a school that helps develop their children both academically and spiritually. They are paying the school to help them. The Christian school must serve these parents well.

Eight characteristics should distinguish the teachers and administrators of the Christian school. These qualities will go a long way toward satisfying parents and will bring a response of love, trust, and support from the parents. Teachers, staff, and administration who consistently demonstrate these eight characteristics to the students and parents will gain a corresponding respect and appreciation. These qualities are no guarantee against all difficulties, but they do help to develop positive relationships with the parents, resulting in fewer problems.

Spirituality

Your walk with the Lord is the most important key in creating good home-and-school relationships. Parents will trust school personnel who are manifestly sincere in their Christian testimony. Many conflicts can be avoided or resolved if the parent is convinced that the teachers and administrators have an intimate relationship with the Lord and mean to do good for their child.

The fruit of the Spirit must be consistently evident in your life. Galatians chapter 5 lists nine evidences of the Spirit-controlled life: "But the fruit of the Spirit is love, joy, peace, longsuffering, gentleness, goodness, faith, meekness, temperance: against such there is no law" (vv. 22-23). What an awesome description of what the Christian will look like as he allows the Holy Spirit to control his life!

Consider the difference between the fruit of the Spirit and the works of the flesh:

> Now the works of the flesh are manifest, which are these; adultery, fornication, uncleanness, lasciviousness, idolatry, witchcraft, hatred, variance, emulations, wrath, strife, seditions, heresies, envyings, murders, drunkenness, revellings, and such like: of the which I tell you before, as I have also told you in time past, that they which do such things shall not inherit the kingdom of God." (Galatians 5:19-21)

What a contrast between works (vv. 19-21) and fruit (vv. 22-23)! Fruit is the result of a living union. A machine may produce works, but it will never produce fruit. Even the law produces works, but God calls them "dead works" (Hebrews 9:14). The law could never produce the wonderful, gracious fruit described in verses 22-23. If the teacher and administrator desire to show these qualities in their lives, they must allow the Holy Spirit to control them. Christian character comes from within, by the power of the Spirit. The Spirit seeks to develop the qualities of Christ in His people (Romans 8:29; 12:1-2). The Christian must "walk in the Spirit, and [he] shall not fulfill the lust of the flesh" (Galatians 5:16).

Walking in the power of the Spirit will produce in your life all of the fruit of the Spirit, one by one and little by little. Galatians 5 continues with this exhortation: "If we live in the Spirit"—this is salvation, being made alive by the Spirit—"let us also walk in the Spirit"—this is sanctification, allowing the Spirit to command and control your life. "Walking in the Spirit" is not some emotional experience, detached from everyday life. It is the daily experience of the believer who feeds on the Word, prays, and obeys what the Bible says. Powerful collaboration with parents demands that the fruit of the Spirit be evident in your life.

Notice that the first fruit listed is love. Do your students and parents see that quality in you? When parents know that you love them and their children, they are much more willing to work with you. The Bible says, "When a man's ways please the Lord, he maketh even his enemies to be at peace with him" (Proverbs 16:7). The parents are not the enemy! However, if this truth applies to "even his enemies," certainly it will also apply to your close allies, the parents. Sometimes a teacher shows the opposites of love, joy, and peace. Negative attitudes hinder the essential home-school alliance. The attitudes of Spirit-filled teachers and administrators will allow them to enjoy successful ministry with parents and students.

Communication

Parents want to be informed of everything that affects their children. Keep them well posted on upcoming school activities. If a student is having difficulties with behavior or academics, the wise teacher will get the parents involved early in the process of remedy. Let your communication be proactive. It is always better for you to call the parents than for the parents to call you. If a problem has long been developing, there is no excuse for giving the parents short warning. The goal is "no surprises": no surprises in semester grades and no surprises in major disciplinary actions. The administrator should be informed of these forewarning communications so that he or she can effectively support the teacher.

The staff should proactively and consistently attempt to communicate about positive things as well as areas of concern. When you have already offered encouragement and have sent home good news, your communication about problems will be received more readily.

Parents will have confidence in school personnel who are both approachable and available for communication. School personnel should return telephone calls or answer email promptly—the same day if at all possible. However, if you attend the same church with a school family, it is best to avoid approaching them at church about school problems. Let the church meeting be a time of worship and encouragement. Have the self-discipline to deal with school problems at another time.

Teachers can use the following to be effective in communication with parents:

- Notes
- Telephone calls
- Email
- Scheduled conferences
- Impromptu sessions before or after school

Some ideas for administrators include the following:

- Weekly communication about school events
- Monthly or quarterly newsletter
- Website with a place for teachers to post the homework and for the school office to present important issues and upcoming events for the parents
- Telephone calls, notes and meetings

By using the technology of the twenty-first century, communication should be an easy task. However, there are some special cautions in order for email. People tend to read email hastily, and it tends to be a cold, impersonal format. Email is a good way to communicate a few neutral facts, like the time and place of an upcoming event, but it is a poor way to deal with problems. The best communication comes when you meet with people in person. Your facial expression and tone of voice can more fully convey both the meaning of your words and the attitude of your heart. Both parties will express more detail verbally than they are likely to do in writing, and the immediate interchange allows clarification and correction of misunderstandings between both parties. The telephone is almost as good, giving immediacy and tone of voice, and occasionally is better because it avoids the time for parents' emotions to build up in anticipation of an appointment.

The teacher and administrator will increase the effectiveness of their collaboration with school families if they are committed to consistent, clear, and Christlike communication.

Standards

One distinctive of the Christian school has been the attempt to establish and maintain high standards of conduct, academics and appearance as part of developing Christlike character. The parents who share your goal of developing Christlikeness in students will, generally, be grateful for high standards. In many cases, the parents have selected your school because of the high standards.

Sometimes, however, parents want the *product* of the Christian school, not realizing that standards are essential to the *process* of producing Christlike character. It is important to be very clear about the standards of the Christian school during the enrollment interview. Focus on the positive goals as you talk about standards, but the parents and students should clearly understand what will be expected of them. Sometimes parents believe in the process of character development—until their child gets involved in some corrective aspect of the "process." You must continually teach, reaffirm, and encourage parents about the essential role of high standards in high accomplishment.

Remember that high academic expectations—and the teaching which helps students accomplish those high goals—are distinctively Christian too. "Whatsoever thy hand findeth to do, do it with thy might!" (Ecclesiastes 9:10) The Christian school must possess an academically stimulating atmosphere. This culture of excellence takes time to develop. It also takes a dedicated faculty and staff, and these people require administrative support. The teacher must be demanding in his or her expectations of the students and, at the same time, sensitive to the various levels of student ability. The excellent teacher sets high hurdles, and provides hurdle helps. High academic standards keep the parents enthusiastic about the school, and this enthusiasm enhances their commitment to working with the school.

The "moving world principle" is now affecting the standards of some Christian schools. This problem comes when an individual or group focuses on the evil of the world and determines to be better than the bad things in the world. Twenty years ago they were "two steps closer" to God than the world. Now the worldly standards are ten steps lower than they were before, and the Christian caught by the moving world principle is still just two steps better than the world—but several steps below the "worldly average" of twenty years ago. Christians do not set their standards by reference to the world. If people keep their focus on biblical goals and expectations, "looking unto Jesus, the author and finisher of our faith" (Hebrews 12:2), they are less likely to be sucked downward with the sinking world. The Christian's point of reference makes the difference. The goal is always to be like Christ, not to be better than the worldly system.

The trend of standards is naturally downward. The public schools have been lowering the standards of dress and conduct for many years. Unfortunately, many Christian schools are following in the footsteps of the public schools. Some Christian schools also reflect the increasing worldliness of the church. The natural gravity of the fleshly mind pulls standards downward. The price of high standards, as well as of freedom, is eternal vigilance. Many Christian schools are demanding less of their students, especially in the areas of dress, conduct, and attitude. Many students and parents choose the path of least resistance. That choice is a loss for them and for the cause of Christ. Yet, you must keep your goals clear. You are not accountable for the decisions of others; you are accountable for the school or the classroom that God has entrusted to you. Be positive. Make your school the most wonderful place it can be. Keep instructing parents and students why standards are important. But be faithful to the Lord, even if your enrollment suffers.

The Christian school does not exist for its standards; it exists to support the parents in their goal of developing Christlikeness in young people. The standards are just one of the means toward that end. The high standards of a Christian school are positive expressions of love. They are the practical application of concern for the child as a whole person. Keep that perspective as you lead, and keep that perspective in front of your students and families.

Control

Every good teacher is an effective disciplinarian. As parents place their children into the Christian school, they expect that the teachers will be able to control the class well. The teacher must have good classroom order if he or she is to be successful. Many unnecessary and uncomfortable confrontations with parents can be avoided if the teacher has established control.

Parents are pleased when discipline is simple, fair, and consistent. The teacher must make the regulations for the classroom easy to understand and remember. It is usually best to express the necessary behaviors in four or five broad rules. The student is better able to remember four or five items than a list of twenty-five. The teacher will be more likely to remember and enforce a more limited number of items as well!

There is a balance in knowing how much to consult with parents or to bring in administrative backup. The wise teacher will do these things; they are part of the necessary communication. However, if a teacher depends on regular administrative and parental help to maintain the classroom, it may be an indication that the teacher's control is unsatisfactory. The administrator should certainly be a support to a classroom teacher. The parents should also be supportive. But the teacher has the primary responsibility for what happens in the classroom.

Competence

Parents will support the school if they believe that the teachers and staff are competent professionals. Teachers earn parents' confidence by proficiency in the subject matter, accurate and timely correction and return of tests and assignments, and overall organization. The administration earns confidence by compassion, consistency, and preparation.

Students will often pattern their lives after someone they respect. This respect may come because a competent teacher or administrator is knowledgeable, resourceful, and obviously concerned for their well-being. Christian educational leaders have another level of motivation to achieve competence: they will be judged by a stricter standard. The Bible states, "My brethren, be not many masters [teachers], knowing that we shall receive the greater condemnation" (James 3:1-2). The Bible also suggests that the teacher's degree of competence can set an upper limit on the students' achievement: "The disciple is not above his master: but every one that is perfect shall be as his master" (Luke 6:40).

The little extras manifest confidence-inspiring competence. The effective, competent teacher constantly evaluates and improves his performance. It has been said, "He who lectures by the yard usually teaches by the inch." By contrast, Sobel and Maletsky (1975, p. 2) describe the master teacher this way:

A teacher must know his stuff.

He must know the students he intends to stuff.

Above all, he must stuff them artistically.

The great teacher constantly looks for new methods and tools to communicate biblical truth and academic content more effectively. Parents and students will overlook some areas of personal weaknesses in a teacher who can make the subject come alive. If the classroom atmosphere is filled with energy and excitement, the motivation for learning will increase, and the teacher is well on his way to avoiding other problems.

The competent administrator plans and prepares diligently. He or she does not put off difficult decisions or conferences, but accepts these as chances to see God at work and deals with each in its own right time. Some things need to be dealt with quickly. Sometimes it is best to wait, even though the waiting is uncomfortable. In managing any organization, there will be unexpected problems. One mark of a good administrator is that even these things become input for planning, as best one can, for the next unexpected event. Good school leaders do not live in a constant mode of crisis management.

The cause of Christ is too important to entrust the training of the next generation to incompetent leaders. If a teacher has significant weaknesses but does not show a willingness to improve, a conversation with the administrator about the teacher's future may be in order. The administrator who does not effectively administrate needs to talk with his or her leadership, whether that is a pastor or a school board, about the problems and possible remedies.

Everyone has his Elijah days. Remember 1 Kings chapter 19? Being physically and emotionally drained, Elijah thought that he was the only one left serving God. He asked God to let him die. But God had other plans. God's first answer was rest, good nutrition, and time alone with God. Some people believe that Elijah had also made a mistake in leaving his servant, perhaps Elisha, behind. He needed godly counsel and encouragement. God did not want Elijah to quit. Nobody starts out great, and the best teachers and administrators have weaknesses. Do not quit hastily: the cause of Christian education cannot afford to lose good people. Still, be honest with yourself and be willing to change.

The competence of teachers and administrators earns the confidence of parents and increases their cooperation.

A Teachable Spirit

The wise administrator or teacher will seek the parents' input. Although individual parents should not gain undue influence in the school, there is a need for parental input. Not only will the school leaders gain valuable insights, but also parents who know that their comments are genuinely welcome develop a greater sense of teamwork with the school.

The Christian teacher should be unafraid of having parents visit the classroom. The teacher should seek the opinions and ideas of others in order to improve classroom instruction. Obviously, the competent teacher who is constantly striving to be innovative, interesting, and exciting will be less likely to receive criticism or instructive parental comments, yet parents will be even more confident of a teacher who invites their input. The teacher must remember that parents are responsible before God for their children's education; therefore, parental input should be sought, accepted, and considered.

The new teacher, especially, needs to be balanced in acting upon advice. Parental input is valuable, but not all parents are trained educators. Listen attentively and promise to consider all input, but tell the parent that you will also seek the counsel of your administrator.

The Christian school administrators likewise must create a sense of camaraderie with the parents. Yes, administrators are responsible before God for the running of the school. Yet, administrators are there to serve the parents. School leaders must not be wishy-washy, being blown about by the strongest wind, but they must be genuinely open to comment and even criticism.

Having a teachable spirit is not just the willingness to receive factual information. It is equally a matter of building relationships. A bond naturally develops between individuals committed to a mutual goal. This bond can be called *rapport*, a word derived from the French and carrying the idea of harmonious relationship. Administrators and teachers who achieve this level of mutual understanding and commitment with the parents have achieved an indefinable magic that unites them with the parents and with the students. The school leaders possessing rapport with students and parents are more likely to find them willing to work in godly collaboration. When teachers and administrators reach this state, they find Christian education to be the rewarding experience it was meant to be. With rapport, the teacher or administrator is home free. He or she can do no wrong in the eyes of parents and students. Without it, parents and students will allow very little margin of error.

Every school staff member is a "public relations officer" for himself or herself as well as for the school. It is the responsibility of each teacher or administrator to build relationships. No one can do this on behalf of someone else.

Sometimes helpful information comes in hurtful tones. Your attitude is the key, not the attitudes of others. Long before you achieve rapport with parents, you must genuinely welcome their input—whatever tone of voice they use. You are not there to prove yourself right; you are there to do right. A simple formula for handling criticism is summed up in the acrostic, LET.

Listen
Evaluate
Take action.

LET God speak to you through the advice of others. *Listen* actively, probing what a person says, asking questions to gain the full picture. *Evaluate.* You do not have to decide immediately. Sometimes it takes time to consider new ideas. However, do not postpone a decision unnecessarily. *Take action.* That "action" may be to change what you are doing. It may also mean that, after careful listening and evaluation, you decide that nothing should be changed, and you continue on.

The English poet Alexander Pope offered another word of wisdom about criticism:

Trust not yourself, but your defects to know,
Make use of every friend and every foe.

A mature person recognizes that "faithful are the wounds of a friend" (Proverbs 27:6), but it takes a *very* mature person to make good use of criticism offered in an unfriendly manner. The

Christian school leader should be striving to be just that mature, or to express it another way, to be that secure in Christ.

Humility

Administrators and teachers should be sensitive concerning errors they make throughout the year and humbly make them right with the students and parents involved. The Christian educator knows that he or she is not perfect, and the parents and students *certainly* know it. You gain credibility and cooperation as you honestly admit mistakes and correct them.

Humility is also part of that approachable attitude which encourages parental input and builds trust.

Compassion

Parents will quickly sense whether the school staff are concerned for their students. The students also know who cares for them. Words cannot long disguise the heart. Even heartfelt words soon ring hollow without action. You begin to build strong home-and-school relationships as you consistently show love, care, concern, and compassion. It is true that "they do not care how much you know until they know how much you care!" There is absolutely no replacement for compassion.

The Bible is replete with references to compassion:

- *He hath made his wonderful works to be remembered: the Lord is gracious and full of compassion.* (Psalm 111:4)
- *Unto the upright there ariseth light in the darkness: he is gracious, and full of compassion, and righteous.* (Psalm 112:4)
- *The Lord is gracious, and full of compassion; slow to anger, and of great mercy.* (Psalm 145:8)
- *Then the Lord of that servant was moved with compassion, and loosed him, and forgave him the debt.* (Matthew 18:27)

It is natural to be thankful for these verses which speak of God's compassion. Consider also this principle: "With what measure ye mete, it shall be measured to you again" (Luke 6:2). This makes the following passages about the need to show compassion to one another just as important as the verses about God's compassion:

- *Finally, be ye all of one mind, having compassion one of another, love as brethren, be pitiful, be courteous.* (1 Peter 3:8)
- *And of some having compassion, making a difference.* (Jude 22)
- *And, ye masters, do the same things unto them, forbearing threatening; knowing that your Master also is in heaven; neither is there respect of persons with him.* (Ephesians 6:9)

That last clause is especially sobering, "neither is there respect of persons with him," especially when considered in conjunction with the principle of stricter judgment for leaders: "My brethren, be not many masters, knowing that we shall receive the greater condemnation" (James 3:1).

The educational leader must exercise great care in what is said—and the manner in which it is said. "For in many things we offend all. If any man offend not in word, the same is a perfect man, and able also to bridle the whole body" (3:2).

Compassion and love can be demonstrated in many ways. As teachers and administrators are patient, forgiving, kind, interested, and pleasant toward each student, the students and parents will be confident that they have genuine compassion.

Discipline calls for special compassion. Teachers and administrators must correct students consistently, but it is critical that the correction take place against a backdrop of compassion. Balance between authority and humility must be exercised when working with students and parents. When you must deal correctively with students and parents, they are more likely to accept instruction if you bring it as a humble servant of the Lord.

John Goetsch and Mark Rasmussen tell the following story of compassion:

> Years ago, the pastor of a fair-sized church had a huge problem—a Sunday school class of seventh-grade boys! This group of junior high boys had terrorized several teachers, and the word was out. No one wanted to teach this class. The pastor prayed earnestly for a teacher and scanned the membership list in desperation. Surely there was someone that could take this class. One morning, he remembered a man shaking his hand some months before and volunteering to do anything the pastor might need. However, he was a relatively new Christian and had never been trained to teach. Besides, he was not outgoing and was not very good with words. But the pastor couldn't seem to get this man out of his mind. He hated to ask him, but there were no other options. The man was shocked by his pastor's request, and expressed his unworthiness and inadequacy, but agreed to give it a try with the Lord's help. The church and pastor watched carefully, hoping that these boys would not destroy the faith of this inexperienced and untrained teacher. To their amazement, the class began to grow! The boys eagerly came with their lessons completed, Bibles in hand, and memory verses ready to recite. Their voices filled the entire Sunday school wing as they sang the choruses each week. One Sunday, the pastor stood outside the door and listened as the teacher weakly stumbled through the Bible lesson while the boys listened with respectful attention. That day the pastor called the Sunday school

teacher into his office. He expressed his appreciation for the fine job he was doing and inquired about what it was that had made such a difference in these young lives. As the pastor continued to probe, he noticed that the man held in his lap a small black notebook along with his Bible. The pastor asked if he might take a look at this "lesson book." Reluctantly, the man obliged. As the pastor opened the book, he saw that each page was dedicated to one of those seventh grade boys. There was a photograph taped in the upper right-hand corner with a name beneath it. Then, neatly listed on the page, were addresses, phone numbers, the name of each boy's school, his parents' names, his hobbies, and his favorite candy. The pages were brittle, having been soaked by the tears of this praying Sunday school teacher who had won the hearts of these mischievous and hardened boys—not with skill or knowledge, but with love! (pp. 34-35)

You can please the parents you serve and maintain their support as you

- Continue your own spiritual growth
- Communicate consistently and clearly to the parents
- Maintain high standards
- Effectively control the classroom
- Demonstrate a high degree of competence
- Encourage the input of the parents
- Serve with humility
- Demonstrate great compassion

Remember, the teacher is responsible for how he or she is perceived!

References:

Goetsch, J., & Rasmussen, M. (n.d.) *Mentoring and modeling*. Textbook Edition. Lancaster, CA: Revival Books.

Sobel, M., & Maletsky, D. (1975). *Teaching mathematics: A sourcebook of aids, activities, and strategies*. Upper Saddle River, NJ: Prentice Hall.

Dealing with Difficult People
The servant of the Lord must not strive

That first phone call from an angry parent—did it take you by surprise? You may have entered the Christian school ministry with a few unstated—and ill-founded—expectations. By now you realize that even in full-time Christian work you will deal with people problems, and you will deal with problem people.

This reality should not be a surprise.

Even in the first century, Paul had to give Timothy instruction on how to deal with difficult people. Paul's divinely inspired formula, given in the first epistle to Timothy, is still a practical guide.

Respond Kindly, Not "In-kind"

And the servant of the Lord must not strive; but be gentle unto all men, apt to teach, patient. (1 Timothy 2:24)

Leadership, even *Christian* leadership, is not always known for kindness. Does your attitude reflect your humble status as a servant? Are you gentle and patient? Or do you have the big-shot mentality that naturally stirs up strife?

This humble servant's attitude is not a wishy-washy "love" with no anchor in principle. It is a matter of providing biblical leadership, but doing it in a manner empowered by the grace of God. Biblical convictions presented and maintained with compassion produce Christlikeness in young people. The compassion in that formula also tends to build cooperation with parents and young people alike.

Consider, "the servant of the Lord." Christian educators are servants of the Servant who washed the dirty feet of those who were about to fail Him. Likewise, you should not expect to be appreciated, but you should expect to deal with dirty-feet attitudes. Responding to people in anger shows that you believe that someone is interfering with your rights, perhaps your right to respect as an authority. Responding in fear indicates a failure to trust God to enable you to handle the situation. These are natural responses, but God calls you to seek His help for the supernatural.

"The servant of the Lord must not strive." First, do not misread this exhortation. It does not say that you should run away from all interpersonal conflict. It carries more the idea that you should not be looking for a fight. You are not walking into this situation with your fists up. Your hands are open to receive a brother or sister with kindness. "A soft answer turneth away wrath: but grievous words stir up anger" (Proverbs 15:1).

Get your own heart right first. You cannot expect the power of God to work through you when you are still in the heat of angry reaction yourself. Those who fight fire with fire get burned. Whether you have a day to consider how to respond to an angry letter or only a moment to breathe a quick prayer before you answer the person who just stormed into your office or classroom, realize the absolute necessity of being a clean vessel in God's hands. Especially if you can see some area in which your actions or attitudes have contributed to the problem, get right with God first, and then get right with the people involved.

"Be gentle." Realize also that difficult people are difficult for a reason. You are probably not the only burr under that person's saddle, but you are the one on whom he or she is venting *all* that pent-up frustration right now. That's OK. You may have been caught off guard, but God has not been surprised. God has chosen you—"before the foundation of the earth"—to help this person. Do not react, reflecting back the negative attitudes of the person; but respond, reflecting God's loving patience.

Before a conference, consider what that particular family may be going through. Maybe they are stressed about problems of which they have not told you. Some of your families are struggling to put food on the table while still paying Christian school tuition. "Be kind; everyone you meet is carrying a heavy load." [14]

"Be gentle unto *all* men." You may be naturally sympathetic toward some people. You may have an easier time talking with some, ... and some people may just rub you the wrong way. As children of God and as professionals, you must be above the pettiness of reaction or the disgrace of favoritism. Those who are hardest to love give you the best chance to model the love of God. Do not blast people away in a show of anger. "The wrath of man worketh not the righteousness of God" (James 1:20). You never help anyone by anger; you will never win anyone over by anger.

As an educational leader you, of all Christians, should be "apt to teach." The word *apt* speaks of skill. You are looking for ways to skillfully guide necessary understanding around another person's mental roadblocks.

---

14   Thanks to Pastor Jerry Wass for this, his frequent comment, so characteristic of his ministry.

"Apt to teach" also implies work. Every teacher knows that. "The heart of the righteous studieth to answer: but the mouth of the wicked poureth out evil things" (Proverbs 15:28). Take time to prepare for conferences. Make notes. Check out stories. Do your homework.

Another element of this skillful teaching is caution. You should usually not respond to an email message with a detailed email. Yes, you want to document that you did respond, but let your response be, "Here's my phone number. Let's talk." Email is necessarily briefer than conversation, leaves more room for misinterpretation, and may be edited for deliberate misrepresentation and sent all over the World Wide Web.

And be "patient." Do not expect someone to see your perspective and suddenly do a 180-degree turn-around. The emotional momentum of a long-held idea is as hard to reverse as the physical momentum of a speeding truck. Often one conference is not enough. But with patient, loving instruction, even confrontation, God can use you to make a difference. Are you as patient with those who have been entrusted to your spiritual care as God is with you?

One manifestation of patience is accepting people where they are so that you can help them get to where they need to be. You want a "straight-A ministry":

Accept people where they are.

Allow God to work.

Agree to disagree agreeably.

Of course, the same rules have to consistently apply to all. Never will a student body be comprised of families who all have exactly the same goals and standards. In applying the principles of Scripture to life, sincere believers are going to disagree. A mature Christian balance is manifested in agreeing to disagree agreeably.

Another manifestation of patience is reliance on the Holy Spirit. Impulsive leaders—whether pastors, administrators, or teachers—are always trying to make things happen, but patient people do their work, pray diligently, and trust the Holy Spirit to do what only He can do: change hearts and lives. Preach the Word, exhort, rebuke, ... but wait on God. When He burns a conviction into a believer's soul, the transformation endures; but when you impose your will on someone' life, the behavior only lasts until that person leaves your school.

Damian Ahrens, administrator of Tri-City Christian School, tells this traditional Hebrew story:

> As Abraham was sitting outside his tent one evening, he saw an old man coming toward him. Abraham warmly greeted him, inviting the stranger into his tent. There he washed the old man's feet and gave him food and drink. The old man immediately began to eat without saying a prayer or blessing. So Abraham asked him, "Don't you worship God?" The old traveler replied, "I worship fire only and reverence no other god." When Abraham heard this, he became so incensed that he grabbed the old man and threw him out of his tent into the cold night air.   After the old man had departed, God called His friend Abraham and asked him where the stranger was. Abraham replied, "I forced him out because he did not worship You." God answered, "I suffered him 80 years although he dishonors Me. Could you not endure him for one night?"

Could you not endure that parent for one year? Could you not endure that person who is really struggling?

Give Instruction, Not Destruction

In meekness instructing those that oppose themselves; if God peradventure will give them repentance to the acknowledging of the truth. (1 Timothy 4:25)

"In meekness" means that you will trust God to take care of your reputation, even your job. You do not feel a need to defend yourself. You want to clarify misunderstandings, but you are primarily concerned that God be honored. Meekness also has an air of humility. You dare not come across as a superior know-it-all. You must humbly teach those who set themselves in opposition against you. ("Oppose themselves" means "set themselves in opposition to you.")

Separation from worldliness is one area in which school leaders are prone to attack rather than to instruct. Most people, even many preachers, do not understand biblical teaching on separation. If you want to drive people away, assume the character of a haughty dictator. But if you want to be "the servant of God," use this, and all situations, as opportunities to open the Word of God.

Instruction is critically important with young people. When teenagers ask why, be grateful, not frustrated. Questioning is not necessarily a sign of rebellion. Even if the attitude of the question is not right, deal with the attitude and then answer the question with the same loving patience you would have used for a properly expressed question. Children are in the process of becoming adults and are, therefore, learning to think for themselves. Questions are good, not bad. Take the opportunity to explain why some activities are acceptable and others are not. Even if a young person does not agree with you, these discussions are spiritually and intellectually valuable, as long as he or she is willing to submit, even without agreement, on the 1 Corinthians 13 authority principle. Prepare them to make decisions for themselves someday by explaining the decisions you make for them now. If you do not answer their questions, they will ask someone else; and the answers they get from peers, secular educators, and the popular culture will lead to ruin. Welcome questions!

Instruction involves the Word of God. As Jim Berg, author of *Changed into His Image,* put it, "If, when facing a problem of living, you don't think of the solution in actual Bible words, you are going to lean to your own understanding." Even if your own understanding does not lead to a completely wrong answer, it misses the power of God, at least. The Holy Spirit uses the Word of God to change lives.

Yes, some will ultimately reject the truth, but some will accept it. You will also find that some of those young people whom you could not convince now will come back to you years later to let you know how God used your instruction later in their lives. Do not drive them away.

Work for Repentance and Recovery

And that they may recover themselves out of the snare of the devil, who are taken captive by him at his will. (1 Timothy 2:26)

Realize this: people are not the enemy. The unruly student is not the enemy. The parent who is undermining your authority is not the enemy. They have been taken in the snare of the devil, and God wants to rescue them. Your kindness, love, and earnest words of exhortation can be part of someone's escaping the trap of Satan.

This work is not about you. It is all about God working in the lives of others, and you get to be a part of it. It is God who gives repentance, and when God is in the equation, there is power for life change.

As you work with people, some will respond, and some will not. Remember that God is not finished with them, even if they leave your school. Never slam a door shut. You may have an opportunity to help that family later. When restored fellowship follows repentance and recovery, that fellowship is some of the sweetest.

Do not quit so soon that you miss the harvest. Do not run away from problem people. No matter where you run, the same people are already there! It's always too soon to quit.

Some Practical Methods

Listen

First, have difficult conferences in a private place. If you are initiating the meeting, it is easy to plan for privacy. If you are accosted in a public area, ask, "Could we talk in the office?" or some other place. Do not allow a parent to make a public scene.

If the person is angry, start defusing the anger with a sincere "I'm sorry."

"I'm sorry that I have offended you."

"I'm sorry that we are not living up to your expectations."

"I'm sorry that this situation has occurred."

Then go on to let that person state his or her situation without interruption, except to ask for clarification. Listen actively. Take notes. Keep eye contact. Evaluate the matter carefully, trying to see it from the other person's viewpoint. Don't defend or argue … yet. There will be a time for attempting to present the "other side" and to instruct, but that time is not at the outset. Often, a person storms in, ready to explode with tension, and then is like a deflated balloon after he or she has spent all of the pent-up energy. It is easier to help someone who believes that you are genuinely concerned— demonstrated, in part, by your listening.

When you can set up an appointment to deal with a matter, and you do not expect explosive confrontation, consider sitting down over a cup of coffee or a lunch (at your expense!). This gesture, which expresses fellowship, can help set the tone for friendly collaboration.

Compliment

Even when the parent is angry, open your response with a sincere compliment:

> "Thank your for your concern about our school."
> "Thank you for being concerned enough about your child to set up an appointment."
> "Thank you for coming to me instead of talking to everyone else about this matter."

On this last one, maybe the parent *has* gone to "everyone else" about this without your knowing it. The Lord may use even your compliment, based on assuming the best, to convict the conscience.

Respond

Pray for wisdom.

There are two good reasons to pray at this point. First, you really do need wisdom. "But he giveth more grace. Wherefore he saith, God resisteth the proud, but giveth grace unto the humble" (James 4:6). It is good to acknowledge humbly, before God and before others, the need for God's wisdom. Second, prayer softens people's hearts, helping to set a tone of two-way communication with that difficult person.

Question.

Probe for details. Seek clarification. Get the big picture. You may need more information later than is apparent at first. Be careful, however, that you do not come across as accusatory in your questions. There is a world of difference between asking,

"What did you do that made Mr. Jones angry," and asking, "Can you think of any reason that Mr. Jones might have responded in the way that you are describing?" Note also that the phrase, "the way you are describing" keeps you from seeming to accept an accusation without investigation.

Do not accept the common excuse, "my child and that teacher have a personality conflict." A personality conflict is just an authority conflict. The child does not have to like the teacher to obey the teacher. Still, personality matters. Maybe the child needs to change, or maybe even the teacher has some offensive personality trait that needs to change.

Sometimes answer quickly.

Some matters are clear and simple, especially matters of policy. Here, you move into the teaching mode. Explain the policy and the reason for having it. Assure the parent that you realize that there are many areas in which godly people draw the lines in different places, but there has to be one consistently applied policy. You do not expect everyone to agree 100% on each rule, but there has to be an agreement to go along with policies with a good spirit, or there will be chaos in which "every man [does] that which is right in his own eyes" (Judges 17:6).

On the "consistently applied policy" concept, expect disgruntled people to have their list of inconsistencies. They will have a list of staff children whose hair is too long, or the teacher who was late to class—and a list of dates and hours when it happened! Some of these matters may become part of the "research and return phase."

Also realize that the most natural thing in the world, in the Pauline sense of the word *natural*, is to assume an "us versus them" posture. "Staff kids," or "kids in your church" get special treatment. Do not be surprised, and do not get ruffled. Just assure the parent of your sincere desire to do the same good, including discipling through discipline, for all. If you can state, without identifying individuals, that you have dealt the same way with some member of the supposedly favored group, all the better.

Research and return.

Answer quickly, but not hastily. Some matters take time to research. You may need to find out what really happened. Sometimes the most important part of this phase is that it offers a cooling off period. Sometimes a good night's sleep changes things wonderfully.

Get back to the parent as soon as possible. If he or she feels that you are just stalling, or that you forgot about it, the emotional charge in the issue goes up dangerously.

Postpone.

Sometimes, even when a situation is thoroughly researched, the time is not right to act. This is especially true regarding a child's feelings toward a teacher. Do not tolerate disrespect, but realize that a child's feelings may change with a little time and with expressions of love. Ask the parent to keep praying with you about this matter as you both keep an eye on it. Leave the burden of a follow-up appointment with the parent, but privately set a date on which you will make the follow-up appointment or telephone call if you have not heard from that parent. Some problems are resolved with time to develop understandings or relationships. Other problems dig deeper into the heart and fester there. Your opportunity to continue to minister to that family may depend on your making a follow-up phone call after a reasonable amount of time.

Resolve the problem.

If a parent's position is justified, apologize again. Name exactly how you have failed, or how the school has failed. Ask for the parent's forgiveness. (It is good for the parent to say, "I forgive you." You may have to ask a second time to get the parent to verbalize forgiveness. This is not common in our culture.) Thank the parent again for his or her patience. Then state how you will fix the problem. Do not rationalize your shortcomings: you would not accept that from a student. "He that covereth his sins shall not prosper: but whoso confesseth and forsaketh them shall have mercy" (Proverbs 28:13). This truth applies to teachers and school administrators too.

If a parent's position is not justified, still start with an apology. "I'm sorry this has created a problem for you." Express thanks again: "Thank you for wanting to get the matter corrected." Then explain why the person's position is wrong. Teach tactfully but truthfully. Do not beat around the bush. Do not leave out the hard part out of fear of a parent's reaction—that reaction will just come back at you later and with more force.

Student problems often reflect parental needs. Many parents have not had the teaching which you take for granted. Some have had little or no teaching on authority, separation, or other areas. "Brethren, if a man be overtaken in a fault, ye which are spiritual, restore such an one in the spirit of meekness; considering thyself, lest thou also be tempted" (Galatians 6:1). Humbly, but with all the assurance that God has called you to this task, assume the role of a loving, concerned brother or sister meeting a need in the life of another Christian.

Parents are often naïve about their own children. Additionally, most people are even more defensive about their children's behavior than they are about their own. Sometimes people would rather not know about their children's problems, but the parents cannot help until they are aware of the need. Teachers, youth workers, and other parents find out things—sometimes accidentally—about which the young person's parents are totally ignorant. God uses others to point out problems which might otherwise go unnoticed and therefore uncorrected. If you are the one who observes the problem, have the courage to talk to the parents.

Again, do not expect everyone to say, "Thanks! Now I see the light." Allow time for God to work after the conference, as well.

Yet, there are times when a parent or a high school student remains in serious conflict with the direction or the staff of your Christian school. This can continue at such a level that your ministry to that family is hindered, and they may hinder your ministry to others in the school. Even if no specific rule is broken requiring expulsion, it is best not to continue having that child or family in the school. This is the Amos 3:3 time: "Can two walk together except they be agreed?" You may have to tell the parents that you do not believe that you can effectively serve their family as the situation now stands. Still be supportive. Help them any way you can as they change schools. But realize when your ministry is ended, temporarily at least, for a given student or family.

The emphasis is on the word *temporarily*. You may often see God's continued work in the life of a young person or a family. You may have the joy of seeing God bring success in the long run.

Difficult people and difficult situations are opportunities. A problem is also a possibility. These situations are always uncomfortable, but after you have seen the power of God in difficult situations, you learn to approach each new difficulty with hope, and maybe even anticipation for seeing God at work.

> *And not only so, but we glory in tribulations also: knowing that tribulation worketh patience; And patience, experience; and experience, hope: And hope maketh not ashamed; because the love of God is shed abroad in our hearts by the Holy Ghost which is given unto us.* (Romans 5:3-5)

Academic Excellence

Building Christlike thinking [15]

The amendment to the state constitution was promoted as a ban on human cloning. However, a little reading showed the deception: the amendment banned implantation of the cloned embryo into the uterus, but it required that cloned embryos be destroyed after 14 days. What looked like a pro-life constitutional amendment was actually a clone-to-kill move promoted by 16 million dollars of deceptive advertising, with 95% of the money coming from one research company that would profit by it. It was all in the subtle redefinition of the word *clone*.

Could the graduates of your school see though such a deception promoted by the media? Are they able to analyze, synthesize, and evaluate information to make appropriate decisions as they engage in the postmodern culture war? Are your graduates experiencing success in the college setting? The Christian school of the twenty-first century must establish academic excellence as a priority.

15   The authors express their appreciation to Dan Burrell and Paul Tatham for several ideas in this chapter which were derived from their presentations at an educators' conference. Thanks also to Linda Kreger for her contributions derived from an article in *Excel,* the newsletter of Upper Bucks Christian School, in which she interviewed Mick Murschell, Al Van Osten, and Phil Larson.

Leadership of the Christian school must know what is being taught in their school, how it is being taught, and what academic and spiritual success rates the instruction is helping to produce. The Christian school of the twenty-first century faces formidable opposition, but it also possesses incredible opportunity.

Decisions That Will Lead to a Thriving Academic Program

Bible Teaching

You can't clean up your act without the soap and water! To put that in more biblical language, "Wherewithal shall a young man cleanse his way? by taking heed thereto according to thy word" (Psalm 119:9). The Bible classes should be the most interesting, exciting classes in your school, taught by the very best teachers.

Psalm 119 gives another clue about what works: "Thy word have I hid in mine heart, that I might not sin against thee" (v. 11). The school should have an organized Scripture memory program throughout the elementary and high school. Inclusion of a selected variety of topics is important, but so is systematic repetition of key verses. This is a major undertaking. It requires development of a scope and sequence for the entire K-12 Bible memory program, but the Word of God is that important.

Biblical Integration

To be truly Christian, a school must deliberately teach every course with an overtly biblical approach. So often, there appears to be a dichotomy between the Bible class and the other academic disciplines. God's Word is truth and must be a part of every lesson, in every subject. Students should see how diligence in doing math homework or doing their own very best job on an art assignment are all part of being like Christ. They need to see how a biblical view of history affects choices people make at the ballot box. In too many cases, biblical integration consists simply of having a

Christian teacher or having textbooks from a Christian publisher. Each teacher should think and teach from a distinctly Christian view of his or her subject matter.

Biblical integration is often overlooked. "Nothing short of a great civil war of values rages today throughout North America," says James Dobson. "Two sides with vastly differing and incompatible world views are locked in a bitter conflict that permeates every level of society" (Dobson, 1990, pp. 19-20). The battle for the next generation is raging fiercely, and the typical Christian school is doing little to engage in the battle. Academic excellence is not only about doing well in college. It begins with the belief that "of [God], and through him, and to him are all things" (Romans 11:36). Students—and their teachers—must realize that Satan and human victims of his long deception want to "spoil you through philosophy and vain deceit, after the tradition of men" (Colossians 2:8). The motive of academic excellence is a jealous promotion of the supremacy of God in all things.

Has your school effectively integrated God's Word into every class? Do the graduates of your Christian school possess a strong biblical worldview? Do they possess an acceptable grasp of the Word of God, and are they able to apply it to everyday life? What do your graduates believe about the critical political and cultural issues facing their generation? A wise administrator will not just assume the answers. This requires ascertaining the beliefs and choices that graduates are making. This information may be determined by a survey conducted in school, shortly after graduation (perhaps six months), and after a longer time (perhaps two years).

Many Christian schools are beginning to grasp the depth and importance of biblical integration. If the Christian school is to enjoy a meaningful academic program in the future, this progress must continue.

Critical Thinking

Critical thinking is the capacity and inclination to think clearly and deeply. It is more than just knowing the facts. Good books alone will not do the job. Teachers must model critical thinking in their approach to both the principles of Scripture and the subject matter which they teach. Then they can challenge their students to do the same.

There is one problem with stating that rote memory is not enough: that statement is so common that it no longer grips the will with a call to action. Yes, teachers agree that their teaching should move beyond knowledge, comprehension, and application of facts. They know that they should lead their students into analysis, synthesis, and evaluation of systems of facts and concepts (Bloom's taxonomy[16]). Yet, teachers feel the pressure to cover a large amount of material, and well they should. It all comes back to balance. Not every fact can be taught inductively or be the subject of rich class discussion, but some should be. If students were led into serious upper-level thinking once a day—or maybe once a week—that would be an improvement for most classrooms.

Ideally, critical thinking becomes part of the culture of a school, the usual and expected way to approach teaching and learning. School leadership cannot mandate a culture, but they can require some things and encourage others. First, challenge teachers about their teaching and testing styles. In doing this, teach about and demonstrate this level of teaching. There are many ways to "expect and inspect." Perhaps you can state higher-level thinking as a category that you look for in formal classroom observations. Teachers could be required to mark lesson plans for one specific

---

16   For a concise discussion of Bloom's Taxonomy of Educational Objectives, see Charles Walker's *School Improvement Program*, volume 1. See also a concise discussion on the University of Victoria, B.C., Canada, website: http://www.coun.uvic.ca/learning/exams/blooms-taxonomy. html

point per week in which they plan to promote that kind of thought. You might have testimonials in teachers meetings. (You may need to let teachers know ahead of time that you will be asking for these. Good teachers may teach this way so naturally that they do not later remember it as anything special.) Maybe you can award a weekly or monthly "Food for Thought Prize"—dinner for two for an outstanding example of teacher-led higher thinking.

However you do it, do something. Work and pray. The devil is a liar (John 8:44), and your students deserve to be trained in thinking past the surface of things.

The church is in desperate need of adults who can reason through matters using God's Word as their guide. In many cases, there are easy choices to be made. There are clear commands of Scripture that obviously prohibit or require certain courses of action. There are also choices that require much deeper thought, analysis, and upper level reasoning skills. The academic approach taken in every class can contribute to the development of biblical discernment.

Academic Standards

The primary goal of Christian education is Christlikeness. However, a Christlike student will increase "in wisdom and stature, and in favour with God and man" (Luke 2:53). The student is not progressing properly unless he is developing academically, physically, spiritually, and socially. Children can be trained spiritually, physically, and socially in the home or local church, but it is very difficult for the home or church to give the best academic preparation. Personnel trained in various academic areas are not usually teaching academic subject matter in the church. Most parents are not equipped to teach every academic subject well. For all practical purposes, therefore, the Christian school is the best institution to teach the academic material necessary for young people to develop academic excellence. The Christian school should diligently develop the spiritual, physical, and social areas of young peoples' lives, but it must remember its special role in academics, since this area will probably not be fully developed anywhere else.

The Christian school must pursue academic excellence and spiritual priorities as it prepares students for future ministry. This ministry may involve leading a local church, or it may include representing the Christian worldview in the arenas of science, politics, or higher education. Intense training in a spiritually sound and academically stimulating environment produces students who are both willing and able to make a difference for Christ in their generation. The Christian school must remember its mission if it is to produce an academically focused and spiritually sensitive graduate.

Curriculum Choices

Christian school leaders have much for which to be thankful today. This generation enjoys vast choices in Christian academic materials. The quality of the materials continues to improve and publishers are receptive to the needs of the Christian school teacher. Still, in some Christian schools, secular textbooks are used even when quality ones are available from Christian publishers.

Philosophy is first. Your curriculum is not a set of books purchased from a publisher. "Curriculum is learning experiences and course offerings that you use to accomplish the goal of Christlikeness in your young person" (Herbster, 1988, p. 1). The books are just some of the tools you use.

Philosophy is first, then people. The Christian school leadership and teachers should discuss how their philosophy drives the choices of "learning experiences and course offerings" provided.

Philosophy first, then people, then programs and properties. Consider how the texts and other academic tools help accomplish the goals of the school. Compare the available materials to the philosophy of the Christian school. Lead the faculty through a collaborative process that will help them understand the philosophical approach that should be taken in each academic discipline. For example, should the approach be centered on the materials, the student, or the teacher? Should the focus be placed primarily on drill, on understanding concepts, or on self-study? What texts and activities contribute best to these goals? How are each of these necessary elements balanced to produce informed, thinking graduates?

Often, loyalty to an institution or popularity of some publisher within a community, rather than philosophy, may drive curriculum choices. Educational leaders should know the strengths and weaknesses of the published materials available. Then they are in a position to develop a biblically based curriculum—in the broader sense of all that contributes to learning, including those published materials—to accomplish the goals to which God has called them.

The wise administrator will lead the academic staff in these important pursuits. The Christian school that is producing thinking graduates is the one that will be successful in the years to come.

Excellence in the Fundamentals

When the Christian school movement began, there was a significant reaction to the "progressive education movement" then popular in the public school system. The public schools had become laboratories for social experimentation. The Christian school rejected the "look-say" method of reading, the revisionist history, and the evolutionary science. The radical philosophical and pedagogical errors of the public schools provided impetus for the establishment of the Christian school movement. They also showed by contrast some of the most important areas for the Christian school to emphasize.

No movement can long continue as a reaction to something else. The Christian school is not just a place to get away from bad things, like the teaching of evolution. Christian school leaders should promote the positive purposes for their labors. It is not just that the Christian school teaches science from a creationist perspective, in contrast to evolution. Rather, the Christian school presents all knowledge from a biblical perspective.

Now that the Christian school movement has come of age, it must continue to focus on the fundamentals that have made it strong. It must maintain its biblical approach in all areas of teaching and training, from spelling to soccer. As the Christian school continues in the twenty-first century, it must continue to promote the basic belief that brought it into existence: the supremacy of Christ in all things, including all areas of knowledge. The wise pastor, administrator, and faculty will give careful consideration to this historic biblical and academic truth.

Growth and Change

However, some things ought to change. The Christian school, even while taking a strong stand on the unchangeable truths of God's Word and adhering to proven educational practices, must be willing to grow and change.

Christian schools should consider areas in which emphasis has changed. Writing skills are receiving increased attention throughout the nation. It is not enough now to teach grammar and literature with a minor nod to the writing skills. Science courses are emphasizing hands-on laboratory experiences for younger students. "Home economics" has become "family and consumer science" to reflect changes in course content.

While the world does more with school-to-work educational preparation, Christian educators can at least keep before their students the need to pray and plan toward their next steps, whether directly to work, to college, or to other options.

Many schools began by saying that they equal or excel their state standards for graduation, but do they even know what those standards are today? Stay aware of what the government schools in your state and district are requiring.

Technology has brought dramatic change to the process of education. Graphing calculators have enabled the teachers of upper-level math and science to lead their students into areas that were formerly college level—and the public schools are going there. Biology students can do experiments involving genetic engineering or gel electrophoresis (separating DNA into its components). CD-based programs allow simulations using student-supplied data for science experiments and civics projects. DVDs and on-line Web sites bring to the classroom things that would be difficult or impossible to see otherwise, and media projectors make one screen available for all the different media.

We are in the Silicon Age. The typing classes of the twentieth century have been replaced by keyboarding classes of the twenty-first century. Word-processing classes have replaced shorthand classes. Additional topics such as website design, graphic design layout, and computer programming have been added to many school schedules.

The Internet is a valuable tool, even though it brings its own set of perils. In many ways it can enhance the ministry of the local church and Christian school. Proper use of the Internet can range from development of a website—to inform, to attract, and to communicate with the public—to an email system which can be used to quickly and effectively communicate everything from grades to photos of last night's basketball game. Internet purchases can save the ministry hundreds of dollars in time and money, and Internet research can be at the fingertips of the students and staff.

While all precautions and care must be taken to ensure appropriate use of the Internet, training in the use of it is important for two reasons. First, the Christian school should offer students the best foundation available for success in their next steps in pursuing God's direction. Christian school students can be the Daniels and Josephs of this society. God used those great people because they stood for right—but the "platforms" which elevated their stand to prominent notice in their secular societies were the platforms of success in politics (Daniel) and business management (Joseph). Second, the school should reinforce the moral teaching of the home. It can help students understand the ethics and dangers of the Internet and to realize the effects that the Internet could have, for better or for worse, on their future ministries.

Those in Christian school leadership must consider the philosophy and ramifications of changes in educational emphasis, procedures, and technology. They must establish a plan for the future that will enable the young people to be more effectively trained for God's glory. Families should not have to decide between getting a "good education" and getting a Christian education. Offering quality education does not alone build Christian character, but it matters for several reasons:

- It shows that the school is committed to serving God with its very best, just as the school wants the students to do.
- It demonstrates to students and families that the school cares about meeting the needs of the students.
- It provides tools that students will use in serving God.
- It keeps students in the school and therefore under its Christian influence.

There is no reason that Christian schools cannot include distance learning and the carefully guided and supervised use of the Internet, with all appropriate filters. The growing emphasis on hands-on science reflects excellence—even if the government schools were doing it first. Leaders in Christian education should identify the very best of current practices and materials and utilize them as much as possible. If a school is going to be successful in its academic program, it must be willing to change in biblically right ways as the culture changes.

Objective Evaluation

Christian schools proclaim academic excellence in their advertising materials, but do they know that it is occurring? In order for the Christian school to improve there is a need for constant evaluation.

Every program, event, or sports competition should involve some form of evaluation. Evaluation should take place by individual departments (science, math, English, etc.) at the conclusion of each year to recommend changes that will be necessary to stay on the cutting edge for the future. Letting the year's achievement test scores lie forgotten in a file drawer is a waste of money and opportunity. But the school can look outside of itself for ideas too.

The faculty could be encouraged to visit neighboring schools. Afterward, the faculty members would write individual observations or a collaborative report suggesting ideas that would improve their own school.

Keep the parents involved in this evaluation too. Actually, it is not very important what the administrator and faculty think about the school if the parents and students are dissatisfied. If families do not believe that the Christian school is delivering a great education, soon the school will have no one left to receive all that excellence. Parents should be asked for their insights. They are a very important source of evaluation. Parents will offer many helpful ideas. The school leadership may not be able to implement every suggestion, but it can probably use some. Graduating seniors and alumni should be asked for their evaluations. Even if people are misjudging some area, it is important to find out what they are thinking. Why is this misperception out there, and what can be done to remedy it? Seeking the evaluations of those whom the school serves does not suggest capitulation on any point of principle. It is, instead, a necessary part of learning how to better serve families.

One by-product of this dialogue will be increased parental satisfaction. First, some will gain understanding of the good things going on in the school. That may clear away some of the misunderstandings and may replace apathy with enthusiasm. Second, people feel valued when their opinions and insights are sincerely sought.

Outside evaluation is also very important. One of the least used yet most effective ways is through school accreditation or a formal school improvement program. These processes are implemented in cooperation with state, regional, or national Christian school associations. The self-study, which is the basis of either program, helps the school focus on different critical areas. The visit of an accreditation team then provides an outside analysis of the school's program, from philosophy to finances, and makes recommendations. These are very important ingredients in producing academic excellence.

Christian school associations and some Christian colleges provide the services of school consultants. These professionals, having educational expertise and godly perspective, observe a school for two or three days and then submit to the administration written recommendations. This input can help the school leaders see areas that need improvement. Just as important, this evaluation can confirm for the leadership what they are doing right. Remember, "Where no counsel is, the people fall: but in the multitude of counsellors there is safety" (Proverbs 11:14).

The most effective Christian schools continually evaluate their programs and strive to make the appropriate changes.

Mistakes That Will Lead to Failure

The study of success is more pleasant, but the analysis of failure is equally important. Christian schools have established a track record, and some patterns have proved to be danger signs. Some choices characteristically doom a Christian school to failure. Avoid these!

Do not lower your standards to increase enrollment. All Christian school administrators face the challenges of balancing the budget. The financial needs of the faculty are obvious, and administrators have a passion to provide for their team more adequately. Administrators also may worry about the future of the school. If enrollment has decreased for a year or two, a panic can set in. Many Christian schools have made changes to the school's standards as an attempt to stop the enrollment slide.

Changes in dress code, behavioral expectations, discipline structure, music standards, and enrollment requirements can completely change the course of the school—but not for the better. These changes may provide a short-term help in enrollment, but they also produce long-term problems. These problems may be very difficult to remedy.

The goal of the Christian school should be to "present every man perfect in Christ Jesus" (Colossians 1:28). The same changes that keep students with weak personal standards will drive away families who share your goal of developing Christlikeness. Why should godly families pay money for mediocrity? Stay true to your mission.

The process and the product come together. Many like the product of the Christian school while they resist and attempt to change the process. Other people like the process until the process involves corrective measures for their children. Holding the standards high, while assisting the young people to reach those high standards, is the only way to produce a spiritual, mature, Christ-honoring, intellectually strong young person.

Always provide support. If students are struggling academically, and if you are sure that your curriculum and instruction are appropriate, provide the help they need and keep your standards high. If students react against high standards regarding worldly activities—and they will, because they are both human and immature—provide encouragement, instruction, discipline and discipleship, but keep on pleasing God rather than men. You are not alone. The Apostle Paul was there too: "If I yet pleased men, I should not be the servant of Christ" (Galatians 1:10).

The Christian school must resist the self-defeating tendency to lower standards. Appropriately high standards, even academic standards, are part of building Christlike character.

References

Dobson, J. (1990). *Children at risk*. Dallas: Word.

Herbster, C. (1988). *Effective teaching in the Christian school*. Greenville: Bob Jones University.

Kreger, L. (n.d.). Technology: Succeeding in the 21st century. *Excel (2)*1, 4.

University of Victoria. (2008). *Bloom's Taxonomy*. 21 August 2007. Retrieved 10 August 2008, from <http://www.coun.uvic.ca/ learning/ exams/ blooms-taxonomy.html>.

Walker, C. (Ed.). (1999). *School Improvement Program: A Christian Perspective* (Vol. 1). Chattanooga: TAKE TENN.

A Strong Music Program
Building Christlike values

Music is a battlefield. Much has been written and preached about the problems which the rock culture has inflicted upon society. Unfortunately, many churches, assuming that the rock music is harmless if given Christian lyrics, have embraced the music that is causing such damage to the culture at large. The result is a Christian culture that is permeated with the worst music and often is ignorant of the best. This is the frame of reference with which many students walk into Christian schools.

Therefore, one of the most important programs in a Christian school is the music program. Music is a fundamental part of the human psyche, perhaps representing one part of being created in the image of God, for God Himself is musical.[17] Students will not live in a musical vacuum. If they are not focusing on the right kind of music, they certainly will be attracted to the wrong kind. The schools producing Christlike students are not only preaching

---

17   Consider, for example, Zephaniah 3:17: "The LORD thy God in the midst of thee is mighty; he will save, he will rejoice over thee with joy; he will rest in his love, he will joy over thee with singing."

against the perils of sensual music; they are also presenting a training program developing discernment and producing quality, Christ-honoring musicians. All students, not just the performing musicians, should grow in their appreciation for good music. Surely this is included in the prayer "that your love may abound yet more and more in knowledge and in all judgment" (Philippians 1:9).

The music program deserves significant emphasis. Next to the Bible department, music is the most important program in the Christian school. Many schools will spend much money, time, and effort on the athletic program. Considering the major emphasis on music in Scripture, should not equal emphasis, at least, be placed on the development of a strong music program?

The leadership of every school needs a vision of what its music program can become. School leaders should observe other schools at fine arts competitions. They can also learn from visiting ministry teams, such as those that represent conservative Christian colleges. That vision, given a plan of development, becomes a goal. One significant goal of the Christian school should be developing students to be effectively used of the Lord in the local church. Such a high goal does not happen easily. Colossians 1:28-29 says it well:

> *Whom we preach, warning every man, and teaching every man in all wisdom; that we may present every man perfect in Christ Jesus: Whereunto I also labour, striving according to his working, which worketh in me mightily.*

Preach and *warn* are strong words. The phrase *every man* becomes emphatic by its repetition. However, even though your *labor* is with *striving*, you are not on your own, praise the Lord! You are *striving according to [God's] working, which worketh in [you] mightily.* You warn about bad music. You teach the good. You labor, but you are working in concert with God's mighty power.

Eight characteristics distinguish the most effective music programs. As these characteristics are developed in your Christian school, the music program will grow to the glory of God, to the edification of students, and to the encouragement of your school families.

The Philosophy of the Music Program Must Be Sound

As in every aspect of the Christian school, a well thought-out philosophy must be established for the music department before embarking on a development plan. Choose your destination, your goal, before you plan your trip.

One important destination is to teach and train young people not only to appreciate and perform good music well, but also to discern the difference between Christ-honoring music and Satan's substitute.

Some people use worldly music to attract the lost for the purpose of giving them the gospel. Nowhere in Scripture is the purpose of music presented as a means to reach the lost. Some of the purposes for music are given in the following verses:

Rejoicing in What God Has Done:

- *Then sang Moses and the children of Israel this song unto the Lord, and spake, saying, I will sing unto the Lord, for he hath triumphed gloriously.* (Exodus 15:1)
- *The Lord is my strength and my shield; my heart trusted in him, and I am helped: therefore my heart greatly rejoiceth; and with my song will I praise him.* (Psalm 28:7)

Praising God:

- *I will praise the name of God with a song, and will magnify him with thanksgiving.* (Psalm 69:30)
- *O sing unto the Lord a new song; for he hath done marvelous things: his right hand, and his holy arm, hath gotten him the victory.* (Psalm 98:1)

Encouraging Oneself and Others:

- *Speaking to yourselves in psalms and hymns and spiritual songs, singing and making melody in your heart to the Lord.* (Ephesians 5:19)
- *Let the word of Christ dwell in you richly in all wisdom; teaching and admonishing one another in psalms and hymns and spiritual songs, singing with grace in your hearts to the Lord.* (Colossians 3:16)

As a solid music philosophy is put into place, the Christian school personnel can become agents of a holy God assisting the young people with this critical area. Music is a very emotional issue. When you touch young peoples' music—anyone's music, for that matter—you challenge the core of their being. While there may be areas of legitimate disagreement regarding exactly where to draw the line, there should be no debate that music can be right and it can be wrong. Music is not neutral! Teaching the morality of music requires not just heartfelt admonition. It also requires carefully prepared reasons and evidence supporting a conservative Christian music view.[18]

One of the important ingredients in establishing the appropriate philosophy is to establish consistency between the standards of the school and the sponsoring church, if there is a sponsoring church. Young people will be quick to spot inconsistencies and to use them as excuses. The pastor and administrator must already understand the perils of wrong choices in music and should give the music pastor or school music director the authority to ensure consistent standards in both the church and the school. The music pastor may want to bring in visiting musicians to speak on music.

---

18   Consider as a resource *Music in the Balance,* by Frank Garlock and Kurt Woetzel, available from Majesty Music (majestymusic.com). A teacher's kit has been created for the classroom and small group setting. Also from this publisher are *Can We Rock the Gospel?, Measuring the Music, Music and Morals,* and *The Battle for Christian Music.*

These guest speakers will reinforce what the music pastor, the school administrator, and the senior pastor have taught.

Establishment of a strong music philosophy is important. Equally important is the consistent enforcement of its practice. If a Christlike student body is the goal, fleshly music must be recognized as an impediment to that goal. Establish clear, enforcable rules about what music is appropriate. Incentives must be established to encourage students to listen to the right kind of music and to discourage the discussion, singing, and playing of the wrong kind of music.

The Music Staff Must Be Competent, Dedicated, and Christlike

Most Christian schools require a certain level of training for anyone assigned to teach first grade reading or high school physics. The music faculty members must not be any different. Too often the music director of the church or school is someone without any formal music training. Sometimes a person with no training in pedagogy or biblical philosophy is placed into one of the most important positions in the school just because God has blessed him or her with the ability to sing or to play a musical instrument.

The church and Christian school music programs must be lead by people of high character and solid, biblical music standards. They must desire to please God. They must either have or be willing to get the appropriate training. Additionally, there are six characteristics that make the music pastor or music director successful.

Strong

The people-pleaser will be in a continual state of turmoil because students and families will often disagree with the school's standards. The director must contend without being contentious, must kindly confront, and must "in meekness [instruct] those that oppose themselves; if God peradventure will give them repentance to the acknowledging of the truth" (2 Timothy 2:25). It takes a strong and steady, yet gentle, person to direct a music program.

Competent

The Christian school simply cannot allow an incompetent teacher to administer this program any more than such a teacher would be allowed to lead the math or science department. The music director and other music faculty must be solid in faith, blameless in testimony, and well trained in music pedagogy with solid biblical music standards.

Growing and Changing

The music teachers must be mature servants of the Lord. They also must recognize the need for continual growth in the faith. The goal must always be to become more like Christ. When any person stops growing, he or she is in trouble. A spiritually stagnant person is not effective in changing the lives of others.

Having the Heart of a Discipler

A music teacher who is teaching private lessons will have many opportunities to disciple young people in a very personal way. If the lesson is taught without expressing interest in the Christian walk of the young person, a precious opportunity is lost. Unsaved musicians can do that much. The Christian school music teacher should be different. The training must be excellent, but the development of discernment, wisdom, and Christlike character should be an ongoing part of the private lesson program.

Demonstrating the Fruit of the Spirit

There is no place for the moody, unstable music teacher in the Christian school. No stormy, storybook Beethovens, please! The teachers must show the fruit of the Holy Spirit in their lives if they are to be influential in the lives of students. Qualities such as love, joy, peace, and patience (Galatians 5:22-23) win the hearts of students. In an emotionally charged area such as music, winning the heart is often critical to winning the mind and will.

Committed to Excellence

Mediocrity is not an option. "And whatsoever ye do, do it heartily, as to the Lord, and not unto men" (Colossians 3:23). Every program of the school must be designed in such a way as to produce excellence.

These qualities, granted, stop just short of requiring that the music director walk on water. But they are good goals for any teacher, and are certainly good guides for the teacher who seeks to influence students in the areas of music choices and skill development.

A Private Lesson Program Must Be Started

A private lesson program will accomplish many things for the school:

- It will provide an opportunity for ongoing discipleship by committed, mature Christian leaders.
- It will equip the young person with skills necessary to minister in the local church.
- It will provide a source of income for the school.
- The diverse areas of the private lesson program lend themselves to different beginning points. Voice lessons are offered primarily for high school students grades eight through twelve. Piano lessons can begin in five-year-old kindergarten and may be private, semi-private, or group lessons. Instrumental lessons in areas such as brass and woodwind may start as group lessons offered in grades five through eight, with private instrumental lessons being offered beginning in grade six. String lessons should begin in the first grade.

The private-lesson program should be self-funding. These lessons are not part of the regular classes, like band or choir. Families choose these as an extra and pay for them on the school bill in addition to tuition and other fees.

The whole program cannot be started at once. The Lord must send the right people—and the administrator must be looking for the right people—one area at a time. The funding gained through the early stages will support the step-by-step development of the music program, including hiring additional staff.

A Strong Foundation Must Be Established

A successful music program results from a plan of sequential development of student skills, a "feeder program." A strong elementary music program is a prerequisite to a quality program in the high school. No level is more or less important than any other level. You need every rung of the ladder.

Elementary Classroom Music

Classroom music instruction is a priority. This is for all the students of any given grade, quite separate from the private music lessons, and without additional charge. (That is to say, its cost is planned into the basic tuition.) Instruction may occur in the individual classrooms or students may go at different times to a band room or choir room for this special class. This program should begin in kindergarten and should be a part of the schedule in every elementary grade. The goals of this program should include the establishment of strong, biblical music standards, encouragement of a love for good music, development of the students' musical abilities, instruction in the history of music in the world and in the church, and instruction about the various musical instruments. There are quality published materials available to assist in this program. The class might meet twice a week for 30-45 minutes per session in the younger grades. It could meet once a week for those grades that are involved in the elementary chorus, perhaps fifth and sixth grades.

Elementary Choir, Honors Chorus, and Ensemble

The elementary choir should include every student in the elementary school. The honors chorus and ensembles can be selected through an audition process.

A side benefit of having all elementary students in the choir is that all of their parents and grandparents will be there for the programs. Fall, Christmas, and spring music programs are valuable for communicating philosophy and building rapport with families and for letting prospective school families see what is available to them.

Elementary Recorder Class (fourth grade)

The elementary recorder class should be required of all fourth grade students. This will be the foundation of the band in years to come.

Elementary Beginning Band (fifth grade) and Intermediate Band (sixth grade)

The band director should recruit students from the fifth-grade class. This band is likely to include a majority of the fifth-grade students. Some attrition will take place over the next several years. Transfer students could also have the option of joining beginning band in the sixth grade.

Sixth-grade intermediate band is the natural progression of this development. Some schools combine fourth, fifth and sixth grades for one elementary band.

Small Music Groups in the Elementary

Other music opportunities will be beneficial when staff can be made available. Groups like an elementary hand bell or hand chime choir, a beginning string orchestra (first through third grades), and an intermediate string orchestra will be dreams come true for some parents and children, and they will inspire other families to seek those opportunities.

Many schools do not pay enough attention to the elementary music program. As a result, the secondary program never reaches its full potential. The success of the high school music program is built on the solid foundation of the elementary years. In the high school years, music standards are solidified, God-given abilities are polished, and performance opportunities are magnified.

Start somewhere, start anywhere, but start! You will not begin with a finished product: sequential development, even if you use a different sequence, is the normal experience. The details of this structure may seem overwhelming, but the general blueprint is a good one to follow. Adjustments may need to be made in smaller schools. Seek advice from a music pastor or a music program director who has an established, successful program. Most of these people would love to advise you about your program. If your Christian school is too small to support all of the programs listed, take advantage of all that you can. Keep in mind that it will take long-term commitment to develop a quality music program. The result will be a blessing for all to enjoy and lifetimes of ministry multiplied through your student body.

Development of the Secondary Program

Music classes and groups in the high school extend the elementary program and include new options. Groups may include choir, band, hand bells, and vocal and instrumental ensembles. A well-prepared class with an emphasis on biblical music-listening habits and standards should also be included. The junior and senior high school may provide the same groups and classes, but the level of instruction and expectation will, obviously, increase dramatically as students grow older. Smaller schools may be unable to implement all of the groups that a larger school has, but every school can do something if music is a priority.

The teacher is the key. The faculty hired to lead the music groups and to teach the music classes should be no less qualified than any of the faculty teaching academics in the school. Attention should be given to hiring faculty who are not only qualified but also capable of producing musical and spiritual results. The quality of the performance, wisdom in musical selection, and the discipleship of the students should be the focus of the staff. Even the smallest school can hire capable and qualified music teachers who will develop a quality program. These teachers, offering private lessons, are self-funding. The music lesson fee is billed with the school bill, and part of the money goes to the school, and part to the teacher.

Performance and Competition Opportunities Must Be Offered

Once the training program is in place, opportunities for performance and competition are helpful. These opportunities are not a separate, later set of experiences after years of development. Students at all levels of development need periodic, short-term performance goals toward which to work. The performances, if handled appropriately, motivate students in developing their skills.

The young people taking private lessons should be involved in recitals. Memorizing a piece to perform in a recital is an exercise in discipline that will assist the young person in many ways for years to come. The recitals should be planned by the teachers and should be special occasions for parents and students alike. Recitals encourage the young people to stretch their skills. To prepare a piece that requires hard work is a challenging but gratifying task.

The school programs are always crowd-pleasers! They are also good public relations if done well. All of the divisions of the school should be involved in concerts. There should at least be Christmas and spring concerts and maybe a fall program as well. Parents, grandparents, extended family, and neighbors will come. Programs are a good time to take up offerings for the music department. People are more willing to give when there is a specific project, like a new piano, choir outfits, travel to the state or regional competition, or some specific band instrument like a tuba which may be too expensive to expect a family to purchase. (That expensive instrument remains the property of the school, available for future band students.) Programs are also good times to get out the gospel. The presentation should not be a sermon—that is not what people came for—but the pastor or administrator can put into just two or three minutes the heart of the plan of salvation, relating that message to the Christian school and God's work in the students.

Always enter the local, state, and national fine arts competitions. A Christian school with a proper focus on the development of the music program will allow the competition to be used by the Lord to challenge the students. If your school has not been involved in the past or has not been very successful, music faculty, students, and the administrator should visit as many events as possible on competition day. Seeing what others are doing will sharpen each person's vision for what can be done. Competitions will help your school music program to reach a new level of excellence. Success, however, is not about school pride or student ego. Everyone involved should see the competitions as just one more method for glorifying God now and preparing for the future.

Opportunities for Ministry Must Be Provided

One of the most important reasons to develop a strong music program is to provide ministry opportunities for the young people.

Recitals, programs, and competitions are wonderful opportunities to develop, strengthen, and encourage the young people. However, the most important task of the music program is to introduce young people to the joy of ministry through music.

There are many avenues of ministry available through the music department.

Chapels

Every chapel should include a music ministry opportunity. As many musicians as possible should be given the opportunity to participate. Chapels, being the most frequent ministry opportunity, offer multiple chances for students to overcome the nervousness of public presentation.

Church Services in the Students' Churches

All students in the private lesson program should minister regularly in their local churches.

Nursing Homes

What an encouragement the young people are to the elderly, and the elderly are a blessing to the young people as well. Children who grow up ministering in nursing homes or in home visits to the elderly are more likely to be comfortable with this segment of society than those who do not.

Community Clubs

Civic organizations like the Kiwanis Club or Junior Chamber of Commerce may want to have special music as an opening to a meeting. Try to find people involved in these organizations through whom to make your contacts, but, if you must, just look them up in the phone book and call. These presentations are great opportunities to let the community know about your school as well as being wonderful opportunities for ministry.

Sometimes shopping malls or city governments schedule school music groups to perform in public places at Christmas. This venue offers a way to keep Christ in Christmas as part of America's cultural heritage.

Local Church Services

Advanced groups could be sent out from the school to minister in local churches. These visits are another set of opportunities for community exposure as well as for ministry.

Wisdom is required, especially regarding students who are in your music groups but attend some church other than the school's sponsoring church. Some students may not be willing to miss their local church service to minister in another church, and you do not want to offend their pastors. Ministry trips to other churches should be few so that they do not de-emphasize the importance of faithful attendance to one's own church. Students should know before they sign up for any music group that there will be such ministry occasions. They should also know the dates, if possible. Depending on the nature of the group, you may make availability for these ministry events a requirement for being in the group, or you may allow students to opt-out of some or all trips. It is easier to minister without one of ten sopranos in the choir than without the viola in the string quartet!

Ministry Tours

Groups could travel to another area of the state or country and take a few days to minister in several places there. These places may include churches, children's homes, or other Christian schools. Ministry tours can change the entire focus of your music department by introducing students to the joy of ministry.

In all of these opportunities, the music director should spend considerable time assisting the young people to prepare their own hearts and lives to be pure and available vessels, ready for the Lord's use. Students should understand that they are not performing, but, instead, they are ministering. They are not there for themselves, but for the glory of the Lord and the good of God's people. The music director must also be involved in the early approval of any musical selection and the final approval for performance. In these approvals, the director is checking both for the acceptability of the style of the piece and for the quality of the performance. These checks prevent the school from hurting its testimony, the student performers from being embarrassed, and the level of technical proficiency from being compromised.

Commitment to a Biblical Product Must Be Maintained

The music program of the Christian school must always keep its focus on the ultimate mission: developing Christlikeness in students. Godly musicians are special people. They humbly serve the Lord, are excellently trained, desire to please God with their talents, and want to serve God in their local churches.

One of the perils of the development of a quality program is the possibility of pride. As the quality increases, so the opportunity increases for Satan to use a good thing to develop pride in the hearts of the students and teachers. All the leadership, from the school administrators to the private lesson teachers, must remind themselves and their students that talents are gifts from God, developed by others, and usually supported by parents:

> For who maketh thee to differ from another? and what hast thou that thou didst not receive? now if thou didst receive it, why dost thou glory, as if thou hadst not received it? (1 Corinthians 4:7)

As the Christian school maintains an appropriate biblical focus, a strong and vibrant music program will grow, and God will receive the glory for the great things He has done (1 Corinthians 10:31).

The Athletic Program's Highest Goal

Building Christlike character

The athletic program in a Christian school can be one of the most effective ways of developing Christlike character in students and for advertising the school to the community. It can also be very destructive to Christian character and to the school's testimony if it lacks strong, biblically oriented leadership.

Any school can have an athletic program that contributes to the development of Christlike character, but in no school will it just happen on its own. Strong, long-term leadership is required to build and maintain a quality athletic program. There is no one personality type required for athletic leadership, but certain biblical imperatives distinguish the leaders of superior programs. From these Bible-based emphases proceed the characteristics which consistently distinguish the most effective Christian school athletic programs.

The Foundation Must Be Biblical

The philosophy of the athletic program must be Bible-based. As in every area of ministry, philosophy is first. The purpose of any aspect of the Christian school must have at its core "the perfecting of the saints, for the work of the ministry, for the edifying of the body of Christ" (Ephesians 4:12). Every decision made by the coaches and administrators regarding the Christian school athletic program must be made in the light of God's Word.

Leaders in Christian education must get past trite phrases, long divorced from original ideals. They must dig below the blithe assumption that all is well and examine their athletic programs. Administrators commonly say that they value the sportsmanship award above the first-place trophy, but how much enthusiasm shines in the administrators countenance when that sportsmanship award is brought back from a tournament? Every decision made in the preseason, practice, and ball games must be consistent with Scriptural ideals and should reflect a high opinion of Christ. This focus should be so dominant in the thoughts, words, and actions of leadership that it is obvious to all and becomes forefront in the attention of athletes and parents.

The purpose of the athletic program must further the mission of the school. Do Christian schools maintain athletic programs because everyone else has them, or do they have a biblical purpose? The athletic program must be an integral part of the school's process of developing Christlike character (Romans 8:29) and producing a well-rounded young person (Luke 2:52).

The mission of the Christian school includes the positive elements seen in secular athletics, but is there more? At the low end of the scale, whether in a Christian school or in a secular setting, is the program which focuses only on the final score and tolerates bad attitudes and the self-aggrandizement represented by the "end-zone dance" of some pro football players. Most Christian school leaders are beyond that, wanting to develop character through sports. Yet most secular schools and community leagues also list character development as a goal. For example, the player should not argue with the referee. But why not? A good answer in the secular world is that the player needs to respect authority and work through problems according to established protocols. Good, and those standards are also biblical. This purpose alone would be enough to qualify as Christian character development. However, does this situation also have any application that is *distinctly* Christian, something that is foreign to the secular program? If a player disagrees with the referee, the coach should see in such an event the opportunity to teach the balance of resting in the sovereignty of God while aggressively doing God's will. The coach should teach that protecting one's testimony for future gospel witness is more important than the immediate outcome of a given call. The athletic program must contribute in real and visible ways to the distinctive mission of the Christian school.

The testimony of the athletic program must honor the Lord. Godly leadership will apply Ephesians 4:12—the perfecting of the saints—to every practice, game, and decision. Failure to maintain this biblical focus has produced the programs with poor Christian testimonies. For instance, an athlete must be bold, aggressive, and energetic to win. That boldness, however, is crying out to be translated into the Christian life. God's people should be bold in their testimony for the Lord:

> *According to my earnest expectation and my hope, that in nothing I shall be ashamed, but that with all boldness, as always, so now also Christ shall be magnified in my body,*

whether it be by life, or by death. For to me to live is Christ, and to die is gain. (Philippians 1:20-21)

The athletic program can assist the school in reaching this goal of magnifying Christ, but that will not take place without a deliberate biblical focus. A wise coach will apply Philippians 1:20-21 to his or her program and to his or her own life. With their coach as an example, young people must be trained to be bold in honoring the Lord with their walk and with their talk. This discipleship will be enhanced as school leaders apply the philosophy of God's Word to their programs, emphasizing the distinctly Christian elements, instead of merely applying the best of the philosophy of the world.

The importance of public testimony is one reason for the administrator to be in regular attendance at athletic events. The administrator must know first-hand both the events and the overall atmosphere of athletic competitions. The administrator cannot attend every activity, but he or she must be at a significant number of them.

All of these ideals may be summed up in one goal: the athletic program must promote godliness. The athlete will learn many valuable life lessons from sports, but the most important lesson is godliness: "For bodily exercise profiteth little: but godliness is profitable unto all things, having promise of the life that now is, and of that which is to come" (1 Timothy 4:8). This verse does not teach against athletics; it simply compares bodily exercise to the pursuit of godliness. Many times the pursuit of godliness is the last thing on the mind of the athlete or parent at a ball game. The Christian athlete should be trained to work hard, to exercise in such a way as to be in excellent shape, to study the strategy of the game, and to apply the game plan to perfection. None of these goals are wrong in and of themselves. They simply must take a back seat to the maintenance of a godly testimony for the individual athlete, for the family, and for the school.

From this one foundational goal, the development of Christlikeness, several other major goals are derived. The purposes of the Christian school athletic program should include the following. The athlete will

- Seek Christlikeness.
- Be in good physical condition.
- Develop biblical character qualities.
- These qualities include perseverance, good work ethic, sacrifice, unselfishness, and respect for authority.
- Strive to be the best that he or she can be.
- Measure success by more than wins and losses. Winning athletic events is important, but its importance must be transferred to winning in what is most important in life—pleasing and serving God.
- Do all to the glory of God.
- The athlete must have 1 Corinthians 10:31 as the center of his or her focus: "Whether therefore ye eat, or drink, or whatsoever ye do, do all to the glory of God."

Yes, athletic programs built and maintained on a biblical foundation can honor the Lord. Unfortunately, some Christian school programs fall far short of that goal. As leaders stay focused on the main goal, Christlikeness, they have the effective foundation to develop all the other desirable goals. The Lord Jesus Christ promises His blessing: "*But seek ye first the kingdom of God, and his righteousness; and all these things shall be added unto you*" (1 Corinthians 6:33).

The Coaching Staff Must Be Christlike

Coaches are extremely important people. The coach either implements or assassinates the school's athletic goals. Many a

Christian school has greatly damaged its mission by the selection of a wrong person to be a coach. In contrast is the true story of a father who had been trying to teach his son a certain character principle for some time. One day the son came home from practice and said, "Hey Dad! Guess what Coach said today!" and went on to tell his father all about that same principle … as if it were the first time the son had heard it. That father wisely did not say, "Son, I've been trying to tell you that for weeks." He just thanked the Lord for a coach who shared the same biblical values.

Of course, every coach in the school must be a born-again believer. If the purpose of the athletic program includes the development of Christlike character in athletes through biblical discipleship, an unbeliever is unable to fulfill this role.

Not only should the coach be a Christian, but also he or she must be growing in the Lord and changing. The coach will not be able to help a young person grow in the Lord if he or she is not also growing.

Every coach must possess the heart of a discipler. As the coach is growing and changing, he or she must always be focused on the needs of others. Although the coach should desire to win every game, he or she must be primarily interested in pleasing God personally and in allowing God to use him or her to produce in every player that same life goal. The "nurture and direction" principles of 1 Thessalonians Chapter 2 apply to the coach as well as to the administrator. The coach who is genuinely concerned for the good of the young people has the platform from which to provide firm leadership.[19]

Athletes will follow the coach. The power of the coach's example can be very good—or bad. Rasmussen and Goetch (n.d.) tell of a 1982 event involving the Air Force precision flying team, the Thunderbirds.

---

19   See the development of this passage in Chapter 6 "A Culture of Discipleship."

The timing of a vertical loop required that each of three F-16 pilots keep his eyes fixed on the leading plane. But the controls in the lead jet malfunctioned, preventing the pilot from pulling up at the critical moment, and all four fighter planes crashed into the ground at 490 miles per hour. The coach should live by Titus 2:7: "In all things shewing thyself a pattern of good works." Following a coach who is a good example, many athletes will soar to unbelievable heights. Following a coach with a spiritual "malfunction," some will slam into life problems with terrible force.

Your responsibility as a parent, pastor, coach, or teacher is much bigger than your to-do list, day-timer, computer, desk, pulpit, lectern, or kitchen table. Someone has his or her eyes focused on you! You are the lead jet that they are watching. Young people today are slamming into the world at incredible rates of speed, becoming spiritual fatalities because of wrong examples in leadership. The opportunity is great, and so is the responsibility before God.

Every Coach Must Understand Biblical Priorities.

The coach's priorities will influence the priorities of the athletes. Coaches should be competitive people, but biblical priorities must always take first place. The Christian testimony awards at tournaments are not sure-fire signs that all is well, but they are one indicator. The coach and administrator should be hearing referees praise their teams and fans—and should be deflecting that praise up to the One who is worthy of praise.

Christlike character and attitudes are more important than winning a game. The Christian school should be the most ethical in town. No profane, angry, or disrespectful language should be tolerated on the court at any time. If an athlete shows disrespect to the referees, the coach should take immediate, significant action. The referees are the authorities on the field and court and must not be challenged without proper procedure and unblamable attitude. Coaches who consistently challenge their authorities, the referees, are setting a poor example for the athletes. Coaches must realize the important role that they play the lives of many athletes. Their priorities must set an excellent example, and they must provide strong, biblical leadership for the athletes.

The Commitment to Excellence Must Be Deep

After the biblical foundation is established and a Christlike coaching staff is hired, a commitment to excellence must also be evident. Two opposite extremes are equally bad. First, there are programs that are excellent in the athletic pursuits but lacking in spiritual fervor. Second, there are programs that have the spiritual focus and testimony established, but are lacking in the pursuit of athletic excellence. Both goals—attitude and diligence—are Christian imperatives: "Whatsoever thy hand findeth to do, do it with thy might" (Ecclesiastes 9:10), and that *whatsoever* takes in both the spiritual and the athletic.

Winning games, meets, or matches is a worthy goal. A quality Christian school will establish the goal of being all that it can be for the cause of Christ—in every area. The Lord will use all kinds of life experiences to prepare students for His service, even athletic experiences. Contentment with being less than one's best does not help students grow, and it is not a good testimony in the community. There must be a commitment to excellence that is just as obvious as the school's commitment to spiritual values.

All coaches can grow in their knowledge and skills. The coaching staff of a quality Christian school will consistently attend workshops and seminars so that they can develop more knowledge of their sports. They should read, learn, and grow in such a way that observers recognize their understanding of the game and their ability to bring out the best in their teams. The purpose, of course, is not to bring honor to the coaches. It is about coaches showing a high esteem for Christ by how they serve God, their schools, and their teams.

The facility also should reflect a testimony of God's greatness and goodness. The entire facility should be at its best, beginning with the church auditorium, without neglecting any other area. Most Christian schools do not have the budget to build expensive gymnasiums, but what you have should be the very best it can be. Do not let a budget make you content with mediocrity. At the very least, the gym and locker rooms (if you have them!) should be clean and neat. If this is beyond the manpower of the paid maintenance crew, let the teams and parents take ownership of it—under the administrator's direction. An excellent athletic facility reflects the glory of God.

Keep a positive, thankful perspective. Never talk down what you have. Do not even make jokes about how basic your facilities are. The focus is not "If we had …" but "We can use what we do have to …" Thank the Lord for what you do have, and do not dwell on comparisons with others. When you compare, you always lose, and you breed discontent in others.

In every area—competitiveness, coaching competence, and quality facilities—the commitment to excellence should be evident throughout the athletic program.

The Funding Should Come from Athletic Venues

The athletic program will not be a drain on the overall school budget if it is run well. People expect to pay money for various aspects of sports in today's society and are often willing to provide additional support as well.

The gate receipts, in most cases, should cover the cost of the referees and umpires for the year. If that is not taking place in your school, you may want to consider including elementary activities as half-time events at the Friday night games to boost school spirit and increase the gate receipts. A number of events could be planned, including hot-shot competition in basketball, elementary ball games in most sports, junior cheerleading, and elementary soccer shootouts. There are a number of creative things that could be done to encourage all groups of people to enjoy the ball game, including church families, alumni, prospective families, and elementary students and families. Some sports generate more attendance than others, but the payment of officials represents a significant expense for all. There may need to be a revenue sharing among sports.

A parents' athletic organization can be a great help. This group, often called the booster club, should be able to take care of the coaching stipends being paid to each coach. Ideas such as the following have been used successfully:

- Corporate signage around the athletic courts or fields.
- Corporate advertising in the program given out each game or meet.
- Sale of school spirit paraphernalia such as seat cushions, mugs, shirts, hats, and key chains.
- Concession sales at athletic events. It is reasonable to expect all parents whose children participate to take a turn in concessions.

The booster club needs the strong leadership of the athletic director. It is possible for parents whose primary interest is athletic rather than spiritual to feel that they have more authority than they should. Even if the parents who first lead this organization have excellent priorities, there is no telling who will lead it next. The lines of authority should be clearly delineated, the tasks should be clearly defined, and the athletic director or administrator should remain clearly in charge.

Special fund raising events have their place. Substantial support can be secured through such events and can be directed toward the purchase and repair of equipment and uniforms. It could even assist with larger items such as building a gymnasium. One event that is being used by many Christian schools and other non-profit organizations is a "golf scramble." Individuals and foursomes pay a higher-than-usual price for a round of golf at a nice course, but they all leave with gifts of appreciation for participation and there are significant prizes to be won. The costs are covered by corporate sponsors. Of course, many different activities can be used, sometimes with the help of professional fundraisers who make their living by claiming a preset percentage of the income.

A self-supporting athletic program will accomplish two things:

1. Sufficient money will be available to fund the athletic teams with adequate equipment, uniforms, and facilities.
2. Budgeted money previously used to fund these activities will be redirected to other important areas of need within the school.

The Student Athlete Must Be Balanced

With special opportunity comes special responsibility. Athletes tend to be praised, applauded, encouraged, and lifted up more than most students. Other students, especially younger ones, look up to the one whom the crowds are cheering. Therefore, it is appropriate to have higher standards for athletes than for other students, "For unto whomsoever much is given, of him shall be much required: and to whom men have committed much, of him they will ask the more" (Luke 12:48).

The student athlete must be a spiritual leader on campus and off. The proactive coach will not need to keep the athletes out of trouble. Instead, the coach will constantly look for opportunities to involve athletes in the lowly servant activities around the campus. There must be a real discipleship effort on the part of the coach, and the student accountability should be intense. Violations of Scripture and school policy should not be overlooked. Both action and attitude should model the ideals of the school. Athletes are given much prestige in most schools. They must not be allowed to use this platform of influence to erode the goals of the school. Neither should they be allowed to enjoy the attention if they are not good examples for the underclassmen to follow. Athletes should use their positions of influence to serve God and to be positive role models.

The athletes must also be strong academically. Written academic eligibility requirements protect the athletes as well as direct their influence on others. Some schools maintain a weekly grade check for students in leadership positions, including everyone on athletic teams. Students must maintain a certain average, perhaps a C average with no F's, to participate. The wise coach will talk much about earning good grades, will hold the standards high, and will maintain consistent and close accountability. Coaches should work diligently to support the other teachers and the parents. They should strive to develop in their athletes a commitment to excellence in academics as in all areas. If the athlete falls short, he must not be treated more leniently than others. The biblical requirement of Luke 12:48—greater opportunity, stricter accountability—must be followed.

In addition to the athlete being a spiritual leader with an academic focus, the athlete must maintain good sportsmanship, without exception. This attitude does not come naturally. The coach must not allow a player to participate while violating clear commands of Scripture in attitude or action. The testimony of the school will be harmed and the athletes will not learn the importance of biblical priorities if coaches and administrators do not demand excellence in sportsmanship.

Last, ministry and outreach focus should be encouraged as part of the athletic program. Coaches should be encouraged to model outreach, as they model other qualities. Whenever athletic trips are taken, a supply of tracts should be available, and the coach should be the kind of person who looks for opportunities to give them out. Coaches should regularly encourage athletes to be engaged in the work of the Lord in other areas as well. One wrestling coach, whose team competes with public schools as well as Christian schools, has each of his wrestlers give a tract to each of his opponents after each meet.

Outreach ministry provides essential balance not only for the athletes, but also for all the students. Christian school young people constantly take in information and knowledge. The Bible says that "knowledge puffeth up" (1 Corinthians 8:1). Young people must be provided with opportunities and must be challenged to reach out to others. There is a world in need of the Savior, and there are many hurting Christians in need of encouragement and edification. The quality athletic program will have a balanced and spiritually focused approach.

Honor Should Be Given to Whom It Is Due

The Bible states in Romans 13:7, "Render therefore to all their dues: tribute to whom tribute is due; custom to whom custom; fear to whom fear; honour to whom honour." But to whom is honor due? Athletic awards necessarily honor the whole person. Therefore, a whole-person balance is important. Students should not be participating long enough to earn Most Valuable Player status unless they are growing Christians. The spiritual direction of the program should be very evident through the qualities that are publicly honored. The natural outcome will be to honor the young people who are striving to live by biblical precepts. A spiritual component should be part of any award that is given at a Christian school.

It is true that "man looketh on the outward appearance, but the Lord looketh on the heart" (1 Samuel 16:7). All that a coach or administrator can do is look on the outward appearance for evidence of what it reflects about the heart. The coach must observe the life and take the necessary steps in the ongoing discipleship of the student athlete.

The athletic program of the Christian school can be a wonderful and unifying program that helps athletes grow in their walk with the Lord. It can also be a devastating force in the lives of the athletes and in the testimony of the school. Dedicate yourself to producing Christlikeness in your athletes by developing and constantly maintaining a biblical focus in your athletic program

A strong athletic program can promote Christlike character. Such a goal is not easy, but it is attainable. God will bless a program that maintains a spiritual focus.

Reference

Goetsch, J. & Rasmussen, M. (n.d.). Mentoring and modeling. Lancaster CA: Revival Books.

Effective School Growth

Spare not, lengthen thy cords, strengthen thy stakes. —Isaiah 54:2

The Christian school movement has gone through many changes since the 1960s. In the beginning, it grew tremendously both in the number of schools that were being started and in the enrollment of those schools. That rapid growth could not continue forever. With the maturity of the movement, a natural pruning has occurred. Some of the schools that were not doing an effective job are no longer in existence, and others continue to prosper. A third condition is common: many good, Christ-honoring schools have a stagnant or declining growth pattern and are in need of a fresh approach. If careful consideration is given to seven areas, a school will begin to flourish once again.

Consider Your Enrollment Philosophy

Whom is your school designed to help? This question is one of the most basic considerations in growing a Christlike school.

Some schools have an open enrollment policy. This type of school has very few restrictions. Schools with this philosophy accept students from most churches or even from unchurched families. The mission of a school like this is primarily evangelistic in nature. Granted, a school with an open enrollment policy might grow to be a large school more easily, but with what effect? If the increased number of spiritually apathetic—or antagonistic—students works against the basic mission of the school, i.e., to develop Christlikeness, why bother having a school at all? Consider also the trust placed in you by those parents who enrolled their children in your Christian school believing that you would help them develop Christlike character while providing a good academic education. If you trade off a spiritually strong environment for numeric growth, you have betrayed the trust of godly families.

A closed enrollment is a nearly opposite approach. There are varying degrees of "closed." One example is the school which is open only to the families of the sponsoring church. The effect on school-growth potential is significant: the school's numeric growth is related to the growth of the church. This is not necessarily a bad thing. If you know that God's design for your ministry is a school that ministers only to children from your church, accept the size limitation as part of that design—and pray for the growth of your church! There is more to the story, though. Although the size of the school is *related* to the size of the church, it is not completely *controlled* by it. Usually a school can do a better job of reaching out to its constituency. Effective outreach is all the more critical with a limited group of potential school families.

If you are still formulating that decision about closed enrollment, though, you should realize that a closed enrollment does not assure freedom from attitude and discipline problems. Wherever you have people, you will have problems.

The limited enrollment pattern has many variations. One version is the school that is open to anyone at some level, such as preschool or even elementary, with increasing requirements as students grow older. Early and clear communication with the parents about those increasing requirements is important.[20] Another variation of limited enrollment is the school which is open only to other churches of like faith. Not every church is called to have a Christian school, yet there are parents in most Bible-believing churches looking for help in providing Christian education for their children. The limited enrollment option allows a wider circle of ministry and still protects the basic mission of the Christian school.

Although school growth will be more of a challenge in schools having the closed or limited enrollment philosophies, school growth can still take place today.

Consider Your Philosophy of Discipline

Chapter 8 presented three philosophies of school management: authoritarian, permissive, and authoritative. The Lord Jesus Christ was "full of grace and truth" (John 1:14), and that balance is the goal of the Christian school leadership—to be full of both grace and truth. Grace restores and forgives; truth never compromises principles of holiness. To be "filled with" both is a balance that requires continual effort—and the power of God. When a school approximates that ideal, most students and parents will see the loving concern for the individual even in the midst of disciple-making discipline. Discipline situations are often emotionally charged. Yet, if parents see that the teachers and administrator really care for the students' well being, they are more likely to work with the school, resulting in restoration rather than rejection.

---

20   Chapter 1, on philosophy; and Chapter 8, on discipline; and the section on "Communication" in Chapter 9 all deal with the importance of communicating clearly and early about the school's requirements.

However, not every story has a happy ending in the first chapter. Sometimes the school must expel a student. If that is not done when it should be done, the school may keep that one student at the expense of losing other families who want a spiritually strong environment. Keep your mission in mind, trust in the Lord, and do right. Sometimes even the student who was expelled comes back years later to say that suffering the due consequence of that situation was part of God's work in his life.

Close the "Back Door"

The most overlooked place for numeric growth is the back door. In biblical Christian schools, the dress standards, behavioral standards, and academic rigors will present challenges for many. These challenges are not the reasons for which families should leave. Remember, "You don't want to lose families that you don't want to lose." You may need to ask some families to leave the school, so you must be focused on retaining the families who are positive contributors to the school atmosphere. The following ideas may help you shut the back door of your school.

Be the Best You Can Be

Your academic program should be the best of any in the community. All of the educators in your community should recognize the commitment to academic excellence present in your school. Let people know about the success that God is giving your school. Present your year-ending test results in school mailings or on the school's Web site. It is not difficult to create a colorful bar chart comparing your school's results with national and state averages. Publish honors and accomplishments of your students and staff in your school's newsletter and submit them to your local news media as community interest items.

The fine arts program should stand above the others in the community. Your school should demonstrate a commitment not only to morally good music standards but also to a technically excellent music program. A quality fine arts program will go a long way toward closing the back door.

Similarly, the athletic program should show commitment to both athletic skill and biblical character. An athletic program with such a good testimony in the community is well worth the effort.

The facilities should be a testimony to a great God. While you may not be able to enjoy everything that is the latest and the greatest, you can present a clean, carefully thought-out, and progressively improving facility, all to the glory of God.

The most significant part of closing that back door is the communication of how the school helps to develop spiritual character. Sometime parents desire the product of the Christian school without the process. The administrator's job is to teach parents that the process is necessary in producing a Christlike product. You may lose some families to other schools which are less committed to the goal of Christlike character, but you may also pick up some of the best families in the community.

Train Staff to Communicate Well

Assuming that the faculty is competent, well qualified, and possess the desire to disciple, how are parents going to know these things? The whole staff—teachers, secretaries, everyone—also must be committed to "customer service" tasks such as promptly returning telephone calls, sending positive notes as well as instructive or corrective ones, and working on the public relations aspects of developing relationships with families. Continually remind staff that their communication should feature their focus on meeting needs for young people and developing Christlike character: do not assume that parents are always seeing that as the focus of all you do. You want to remind them of the principles that brought them your way at the start. These tasks are the responsibility all teachers. They are part of discipling families.

Demonstrate your care for families in as many tangible ways as possible. Rosanne Petermeyer of Pensacola Christian High School phrased it memorably: "Is that third grader's lunch box important to you? It is to his mother."

Evaluate School Events

The faculty and staff member leading each program or special event should complete an event evaluation form immediately after the event. This form has two major functions. It shows respect for the faculty, giving them opportunity for input. It also makes the administrator aware of problems to solve from recent events or problems to prevent in future ones. A sample is provided in the appendices.

Diagnose Departures

Ask for the privilege of an interview with every family that withdraws their children from your school. This meeting is important whether the family is moving out of town or going to another school locally. In either case, you may get valuable and candid insights from these parents. These ideas can help you become a better administrator and can help your school to improve as well. For parents who are leaving because of problems at—or problems with—your school, this sometimes is a chance to help people work through problems in a biblical way. This type of conference has sometimes kept families in a school which they might otherwise have left.

A departure questionnaire must be developed to send to every family that decides to leave your school. This is valuable with or without the exit interview. The questionnaire should be comprehensive yet easy and quick to complete. Parents and older students could be asked to rate the following:

- Administration
- Faculty
- Academics
- Discipline structure
- Bible program
- Chapel program
- Spiritual atmosphere
- Communications
- Extracurricular programs
- Music program

The questionnaire should provide an opportunity for additional comments from the parents. A sample is included in the appendices.

A school should also track where students are coming from and going to. This information can help you identify trends that are working for or against your school's enrollment.

Survey Seniors

The administrator should meet with each senior in the spring and ask the following questions:
- What are the strengths of our Christian school?
- What are the weaknesses?
- Evaluate the academic program of the school:
    - Is it too rigorous?
    - Is it not rigorous enough?
    - What were the best classes?
    - Are there classes that should be strengthened?
    - Do you feel prepared for college?
- How is the spiritual atmosphere of the school?
    - Do the majority of the young people have a desire to do what is right?

- What elements of the school have assisted your walk with the Lord?
- Are there things that should be changed to assist the student body in their spiritual growth?
- Are there young people in the school who should not be here?
- Are there scorners in the school?
• What are your thoughts on the discipline structure of the school?
• Are the faculty and administration consistent?
• Please list the schools in our athletic league that show good sportsmanship and a Christlike testimony.
• What is your future plan? If it includes college, where?

The tone of the conversation should be friendly and sincere. You should work from a list of questions and make notes from the senior's replies. Do not be so tied to the list that you cannot pursue important ideas as they come up.

Obviously, a discussion such as the one described here is time consuming. It will typically take one class period per senior, but it could be the most effective time spent by the administrator for closing the back door. The administrator must have his finger on the pulse of all that is taking place at school. The act of taking a survey or conducting interviews does not mean that the administrator is going to let the school be directed by students' opinions. There are obviously many things that the administrator will not be able to change or that he should not change. However, this interview and questionnaire can clarify for him things that are important to the students, thus allowing him to approach these issues in a positive way as he attempts to create an atmosphere that is in harmony with the mission and purpose of the school.

Survey Alumni

An alumni questionnaire should be established and sent to the graduates sometime during their first three years out of school. Although the young people may provide good ideas upon graduation, they may even more valuable perspectives once they have gone on to their next steps in life.

Meet with Office Staff

A weekly staff meeting with the secretaries is a normal way to organize the activities of the week. Use this time to ask what they are seeing and hearing in their front-line communications. The secretarial staff is probably hearing from parents, students, and even faculty. This information is valuable to the administrator who is interested in closing the back door. If negative comments are being communicated by anyone, it is important to know that and to be able to address whatever the issues may be.

Also meet each week with those who are administrative staff members. Administrators can erroneously assume that everyone is aware of and has the same perspectives on opportunities, needs, or potential problems. Everyone must be working from the same set of facts and must be aware of each other's perspectives. "In the multitude of counselors there is safety" (Proverbs 11:14).

Make "Daily Dose of Reality" Calls[21]

The administrative staff should call the parents of two families each week. These calls are good public relations, but they also provide a daily dose of reality—information that could be helpful in closing the back door. What the parents think is very important, because they naturally assume that what they have heard or seen is the whole story. They may not stop to consider that all they know about some problem area comes to them filtered through

---

21   Special thanks to Dr. Rick Fielding for the "daily dose of reality" concept.

the maturity and perspective of a child or teen. Unfortunately, very few people go to the administrator when they see or hear something they think is not quite right. Questions such as the following should be asked in the telephone conversation:

- How is your child adjusting to school? Or, how does your child like school?
- What has the homework load been like?
- Is your child making friends? Or, does your child have significant friendships?
- Have communications to the home from the teacher and administration been clear?
- Can we assist you in any way?
- Do you have any suggestions to make or any help to offer as we seek to be more effective?

Communicate, Communicate, Communicate!

The administrative and office staff as well as the faculty must focus on meeting the needs of school families, including the parents as well as the students. The following ideas can make your school different from the school down the street.

Letters of Encouragement

Send letters of encouragement to students, parents and faculty alike. You could send these letters for honor society induction, class officer nominations, awards received, birthdays, anniversaries, illness, deaths, financial setbacks, or births. As you are expressing your care and concern in these tangible ways, you are producing an atmosphere that families desire and need. Consider supplementing the detention or demerit system with "Attention Slips" by which the administrator can express appreciation for a student that is doing well. Mail these directly to the parents: students sometimes do not carry home even the positive communication, and you want to encourage both the students and the parents.

Weekly Communiqué

A weekly communiqué should be provided to the parents. In the elementary, the teacher communicates to the parents practical classroom details such as upcoming major projects, field trips, the tests planned for the week, and maybe even the quizzes.

School Newsletter

A school newsletter is a practical help and a great advertisement. It can include school-wide events, student and staff birthdays, and upcoming athletic events. Parents will look to it for practical information such as when the bus will depart for a ball game and when it will return. The newsletter can give details of upcoming events and report on recent events—and remember the power of the picture in such a report! The newsletter lets people know that yours is an active school with much to offer.

Monthly or Quarterly Magazine

A monthly or quarterly newsletter or magazine could be sent to the school family and alumni including the following:

- More in-depth reporting on class and school events.
- Educational articles.
- Philosophical articles.
- Practical articles.
- Devotional articles.
- Public relations.
- An alumni section, which would provide updates on the lives of alumni.

Christian school organizations provide ready-made newsletters dealing with broad issues of concern to all Christian school parents. These will not deal with your school in particular, but they may be sent attached behind a front page that is specifically about your school.

If this magazine or newsletter is of sufficient quality, several copies could be sent to realtors to include in their files to provide to those moving into your area who are looking for a quality Christian school.

Closing the back door is the most important aspect of school growth. This relates directly to the fact that word of mouth is the most common reason for new families coming to a Christian school. On the other hand, when disgruntled parents leave your school, not only are you losing the opportunity to minister to their family; but also they are probably influencing others. The most effective way to close the door is to have a faculty and staff committed to biblical discipleship. These suggested methods are just means of discipling. The *actions* of discipleship are not enough, however. When each staff member also demonstrates the *heart* of a discipler, a parent will have a difficult time withdrawing from such a loving, caring, and discipleship-oriented school.

Consider Proclaiming the School to the Community

Perhaps you have a really good Christian school—but nobody knows it is there. Study the following ways to proclaim the school to your community.

Take Advantage of Free Advertisement Opportunities

Local newspapers and radio and television stations may be eager to mention more hometown events. They may provide sports reporting, even sending a reporter and a photographer to your games. The newspaper may also regularly print scores if you develop with them a system of immediately getting scores to them after each event. Some local papers publish the area schools' honor rolls and lists of graduates. Definitely let the media know about awards earned by students and staff, including in-house awards, such as "teacher of the year" or "booster of the year." At the very least, when you communicate with the media, have several points ready to explain the significance of the award and what the individual did to earn it. If you write the basics of the article, you increase your chances of newspaper publication. If you have the right person on staff, this type of communication could be part of his or her responsibilities, perhaps even counting as the equivalent of teaching a class period in a teacher's work load.

The press release is a common means of offering information to your local newspaper to be published as community news. Start with an attention-getting headline which indicates the nature of the event you are announcing. It should be on your letterhead, no more than one page, double spaced. It should be highly focused; avoid excessive adjectives. Use active voice verbs. Be sure to include the date, time, and place of the event and the school's contact information, both telephone and email.

Public service announcements (PSAs) are a regular free service provided by radio and TV stations. Not only are they good public relations for the stations, but the Federal Communications Commission also requires a certain amount of broadcast time be given to such community service. These often show up as "community bulletin boards." PSAs could mention upcoming school events such as concerts, plays, commencement, honor society, Grandparents' Day, special meetings, Career Day, and open house. They are similar to the press release, but much shorter: two to three lines that could be read in ten seconds.

Personal contact helps to get either of these published. Build relationships with real people at these media outlets. If you do not know where to start, call the newspaper or station and ask for the name and title of the public service director or the person in charge of the community calendar. Approach the media with tact, but do approach them.[22]

Invest in Quality Advertising:

- Build a quality sign for the church and school, or for the school separately, if there is already one for the church.
- Develop a quality website.
- Invest in a quality Yellow Pages advertisement.
- Create a quality brochure and presentation package to give to those who enquire about the school.

Notice the recurring word: quality. Do not let an amateur product persuade people *against* coming to your school!

Advertising is important, but remember this: if greater attention is placed on the "proclamation" than on the "back door," the school will simply change the families to which it ministers. If the needs of current families are not met, consistent growth and effective ministry will not take place over the long haul.

Diligently Follow up Each Initial Contact

Follow up is the strategy most often overlooked by administrators. It requires organization, initiative, time, and effort; but it produces results.

A Well-prepared Secretary

When a family calls the school for the first time, the secretary must be very well prepared to enthusiastically represent the school to the parent. The secretary should not simply answer the questions and place a packet in the mail. This telephone call may be the most important call of the day—the parent should certainly come away feeling as if his or her call was that important. The

---

22   Ideas for this section are drawn from "12 Handy Steps for Writing Great Press Releases" and "How to Write Public Service Announcements."

secretary taking these calls must have excellent people-skills. A new-contacts form should always be by the telephone.[23] This form has places for listing students' names and grades, parents' names, telephone and email, and how the family heard about the school. The interests of the parents should be noted ("What led you to call us today?"), and the secretary should focus the conversation on the areas of the school that meets the needs expressed by that family. The secretary should have at hand a written list of the distinctives of the school.

Computer Spread Sheet

All of the data received from this telephone call is recorded and entered into a computer spreadsheet. The administrator uses this to keep up with the status of prospects.

Presentation Packages

A quality presentation package should be mailed on the day that the family first calls the school.

Administrative Follow-Up

The administrator should make a follow-up call in eight to ten days. The administrator identifies himself or herself and asks questions like these: Did you receive the packet? Do you have any questions regarding the information provided? These simple questions provide an opportunity for the conversation to go on to other points that might help the parents decide to enroll. The administrator should enjoy the opportunity of helping parents see what the school can do for their families.

Have an Open House

After a while, the school will have a list of people who have inquired within the last year. An open house might be held once a month. This is an evening for parents to see the school, meet

---

23   A sample new-contact form is included in the appendices.

administrators and other selected personnel, and to hear a brief, fact-filled, and enthusiastic presentation about the mission, methods, and successes of the Christian school. Refreshments are a must! Not only does a spoonful of sugar help the medicine go down, but also people stand around and talk when they have a cookie or a can of soda pop in hand. This is a time for building relations. You should provide an opportunity for parents to fill out applications that night.

Fliers are sent to the entire mailing list two weeks before each open house. The flier should be an excellent portrayal of the school and should describe what the evening will include. Don't forget times, address, phone number, and a map! Include the email address and post an eye-catching notice of the upcoming open house on the home page of the school website.

A follow-up telephone call is made to each family on the mailing list to remind them and to ask if they will be able to attend. A script could be provided for volunteers willing to make the follow-up telephone calls, but it must not sound wooden. These calls require special people.

Consider the Matriculation Process

Once the application is received, the matriculation (enrollment) process begins. The application should be quite detailed and should provide the administrator with an accurate prediction of whether the child would be accepted into the Christian school. The following areas give some hints about the spiritual condition of the family:

- The family's church, pastor's name, and contact information.
- How regularly the family attends that church.
- Whether the child has ever been expelled or suspended.
- Whether the child (seventh through twelfth grade) has ever been arrested or placed on legal probation.
- Why the family wants to enroll at the Christian school.

Be sure to include a pastor's reference form in the enrollment packet. The family fills this out with their church's name and the pastor's name, address, and phone number. Parents should know up front that you will request the pastor's reference. The reference form is mailed from the school to the church and should be mailed back to the school by the pastor or answers could be provided by telephone. It should outline the doctrines that are essential for harmony with your school and should ask the pastor whether that church is in agreement on these points and whether the family is faithful in attendance and actively involved in that church. Allow room for a pastor to explain doctrinal differences. Often there are areas where a church's belief does not exactly match your wording, yet the difference is not significant, once explained.

The administrator will interview the parents (and the child in the case of a high school enrollment). The administrator of the school carries a very heavy responsibility at this stage. All aspects of the interview and reference process will, of course, be driven by the enrollment philosophy. The Christian school should not be known for accepting the students who are rejected by the public school or other Christian schools. There is trouble ahead for the school that is not careful in this area.

Prayer

Are you keeping the enrollment of your Christian school before the Lord earnestly and regularly? As a leader in your ministry, are you influencing those you lead to pray about the needs of the school? It is just as right to pray for students to enlighten as it is to pray for the enlightenment of students you already have. It is just as right to pray for enrollment as it is to pray for your daily bread.

Christian schools can grow today! If serious consideration is given to these areas, school growth will result. May God continue to bless your school as you maintain your focus on pleasing Him with decisions that accomplish the one ultimate goal: developing Christlike students.

References

12 handy steps for writing great press releases (2006, January 31). Retrieved June 18, 2007, from http://www.press-release-writing.com/newsletters/t171-12step.htm

How to write public service announcements (2001, October 17). Retrieved June 18, 2007, from http://www.press-release-writing.com/newsletters/t54-psa.htm

Epilogue

The Refrigerator Box and the Diamond

"You don't need a refrigerator box for a diamond." A colleague of ours has said that many times to one of his daughters. She is sweet and godly, intense and efficient, and she stands five feet and one-half inch tall. ("I'm proud of that half inch," she says.) The "refrigerator box" analogy means that size does not determine value. The diamond, though small, is extremely valuable, brilliantly beautiful, and highly prized.

Your Christian school may be a diamond. If God is using you to develop Christlikeness in students, your staff and students are brilliantly reflecting the light of heaven. There are parents out there praying for the kind of support your school offers, but there may not be as many of those parents as there are parents who are drifting with the flow of the common culture and worldly ways.

Christian families usually want their children to turn out godly, loving and serving the Lord. However, the process leading to that result is often difficult. The disciplines of godliness are hard for the student, the parents, and the school staff. Subduing one's own carnal nature is hard. Training other people is even harder.

The result may be that you have a smaller school. That is all right. You must fulfill the ministry God has called you to, not some other. Rejoice in that ministry! The goal of Christian education is Christlikeness for however many will accept it. Having a large school is not the goal. It is better to fulfill your calling than to waste your days chasing the wrong goal.

A school can be operated with any number of students. It may require hard decisions. If a school grows smaller, it may not be able to retain all the staff. It may lose some programs. Don't focus on the "can'ts." Stay excited about doing what you are called to do—excitement is contagious.

There are benefits in the smaller school, too. I am thinking of one small school in our area. Everybody is needed. There is a volleyball team, and all the girls are on it. All the boys are on the basketball team. Everyone participates in the regional Bible, academic, and fine arts tournament—and they do very well, because the administrator is excited about his school, and everyone pours his or her heart into it.

Be careful not to conclude too quickly that a declining enrollment is inevitable. It is easy for an administrator to blame the decrease of enrollment on a lack of parental commitment or pervasive worldliness. It is harder to honestly ask whether the school is developing a top quality program. Sometimes administrators adopt the attitude, "We are small and getting smaller, but we'll hold the fort 'til Jesus comes." Instead of holding the fort, perhaps they should aggressively charge the foe. This book is all about ways to do a better job, to keep the people who are already committed to your philosophy, and to reach new families who want what your school has to offer. Charging, doing all that is within your power, is more profitable than holding the fort, and it is more fun!

Also be careful not to condemn other schools; that will not help you. Enthusiastically promote your differential advantage. Market to your base! Your people are continually getting the other messages, such as "bigger is better" or "you don't have to be so strict." Keep the big-picture goal in front of your people. Keep teaching and reminding staff, students, parents, and your sponsoring church of the purpose of Christian education: helping families develop Christlikeness in their children.

At the *bema*-seat judgment of Christ, the worthless works will be burned up, and you will be rewarded for those works which remain, pictured as gold, silver, and precious stones (1 Corinthians 3:12). "And the fire shall try every man's work of what sort it is" (3:13). What *sort,* not what *size.* At that point the well-cut and polished diamond will be much better than a large piece of charcoal.

Appendices

Appendix 1

Pastor, Your Christian School Needs You
By Dr. Jack Scallions

The local church was the delivery room for the Christian school movement. Church buildings were modified and space for classrooms was carved from Sunday school wings and fellowship halls across America. Pastors with little or no educational background took their people on this incredible venture of faith because of a personal burden for a Christ-centered, Bible-based education. Pulpits were red hot with strong preaching concerning the responsibility of child-training and the dangers of secular humanism that permeated the state school system. What the movement lacked in quality, it made up in enthusiasm and optimism. Christian school teachers drew sub-par wages and donated a great portion of that back to the ministry. Textbooks were scarce in many areas. Outdoor parking lots served as gyms; lunch boxes and brown paper bags held the lunches; and the classroom often doubled as the cafeteria. There was never enough money. Out in front of this jubilant, tireless, marching army were the pastors. The pastors served in every capacity from teacher to custodian. They raised the money, hired the staff, prepared the facilities, conducted the chapels, attended every extracurricular event, and bathed the entire venture in sweat, tears, and prayers.

Much Has Changed since Those Early Days

We now boast of excellent educational programs complete with graded curriculum, goals and objectives, and testing programs to keep accounts on actual accomplishments. The lone basketball goal in the corner of the church parking lot has been replaced by a multifaceted activity center housing full-sized gymnasiums and spacious classrooms. Teachers now not only come well prepared in their fields but also have massive support teams from all types of associations which provide direction and assistance. The market for teaching materials is a veritable potpourri. On the state and national level there has been a measure of respect given by many organizations and political bodies to the Christian school movement.

My greatest fear, however, is that those men who have ridden point during the pioneer days of the Christian school movement are becoming increasingly absent. In my great state of Tennessee, I can count on one hand the Tennessee Association of Christian Schools pastors who still stand at their original posts after twenty years. Sadder still is the silence in our pulpits concerning the present-day need for Christian education. It has become increasingly more difficult to gather pastors together for school meetings. I have watched as some who never missed a convention or conference in relation to Christian education now send someone else in their stead.

My purpose in this article is certainly not to be critical. After being in the pastorate thirty-five years with involvement for twenty-five of those years in the Christian school movement, I think I know the pressures pastors face today. We all know the murderous schedules and the increased demand on the pastor's time. Each new ministry opportunity requires preparation and management. Many of our pastor friends have left the main road of involvement because of apparent potholes in the road.

Reasons for Diminished Pastor Involvement

Let me suggest seven reasons pastors have withdrawn from their school ministries.

The first reason is the graduation of their own children.

The Christian schools started in the 60s and 70s were started by the baby boomers. Some, like me, were motivated in part due to the fact that we had school-age children. We wanted a school where we could perpetuate our faith in our own children. Now after three decades, these pastors have seen their children graduate. We have gone to all of the ball games, PTF meetings, and signed the last report card. With a sigh of relief, many have said, "Boy, I'm glad that's over!" Perhaps the luster has diminished; for some it is due to the fact that not one of those kids on the playground, or on the ball court, or in the lunch line actually belongs to them.

The second reason is the decline in church attendance.

Many pastors have seen a leveling off of church attendance and for some a decline since the booming days of the 70s and early 80s. Whether true or not, I cannot say, but in many cases the Christian school has been branded as the culprit. Jokes were told such as, "If I ever met a man I didn't like, I would try to get him to start a Christian school."

Number three is the burden of administration and control of the Christian school.

Pastors watched as their schools became increasingly difficult to manage. There has been a breakdown of standards. Constant nagging by parents and staff alike concerning the rigidity of dress and behavioral standards has become the order of the day. Many pastors reluctantly abandon Bible principles to hold onto students or just to have peace of mind.

The fourth reason is unrealized expectations from graduates.

We have all had sufficient time to analyze the end product of our efforts. The expected result, Christian young people graduating thoroughly equipped for a Christian college and eager to serve the Lord, has been the exception rather than the rule. After watching a steady parade of graduates, many without a heart for God or the least bit of motivation toward the ministry, some pastors may question the entire process.

Number five in this list is the need for additional school staff and support workers.

In my time in the pastorate, I have yet to have a serious church problem originated by a layman. But as a pastor, I have seen many disloyal and disruptive staff or support workers bring confusion to the church. With the advent of the Christian school, the pastor's staff erupted into a host of people. A man who had once handpicked a few trusted people to assist him is now faced with the need for a small army of staff and workers. After finding, interviewing, screening, and hiring these folks, he now must shepherd them, discipline and correct them, as well as take the heat from his congregation for the myriad of decisions they make.

Culprit number six has to do with outside intervention.

It seems as if everyone wants a piece of the educational action. Monitors are everywhere and the list seems to grow each year. Fire marshals, asbestos inspectors, health departments, building and zoning departments, Department of Human Services, and transportation regulators, accreditation committees, auditors, and salesmen knock on the pastor's door, more in some states than others.

The last of the list of seven is the constant need for finances.

The school ministry is like a starving beast with an insatiable appetite. Couple that fact with the many variables that accompany the ministry, and some churches have found themselves dipping into the church coffers. Every plan of finance has been tried from missionary support of staff to routine fund-raising efforts. Budgets, finance meetings, and support strategy can occupy hours of time.

Responsibility for the Ministry

Although all or part of the aforementioned premise may be true in a pastor's life, it is my conclusion that he still holds the responsibility for the success of his Christian school in his hand and must have the vision for it in his heart.

The Scripture teaches that the pastor has one basic responsibility: to mature the saints for the work of the ministry (Ephesians 4:12). In order to do so, his job description encompasses five areas.

The pastor is the elder.

By age and by experience, his position is one of leadership by example.

The pastor is the superintendent.

The term "bishop" or "overseer" indicates a person who is in charge and is ultimately responsible for all aspects of the ministry.

The pastor is the preacher.

He is the one who exhorts the people. Those in his ministry depend upon him for a word from heaven.

The pastor is the shepherd.

The very word pastor has its roots in the thought of feeding the flock. As shepherd, the pastor protects and provides for his people.

The pastor is the teacher.

The instruction must be consistent, informative, repetitious, and applicable to people at all levels of maturity.

It is easy to make the argument for the total involvement of every pastor in Christian education based on the five areas of the ministry mentioned above. It could also be noted that only the pastor can meet the criteria so needed by our students and faculty alike. Aside from responsibility, the pastor is gifted in areas that make his participation essential. Rarely will there be anyone in the system who holds a total overview of the complete ministry like the pastor. Whether the school is large or small, the pastor's presence in the halls, classrooms, chapels and at extracurricular events adds importance and weight of purpose to the entire matter.

Getting Personally Involved

All of the reasons to be a part of Christian education have not diminished but have compounded over these past decades. The Christian school is still a remarkable tool to protect young people and families from the destructive elements of sin and to empower them with truth for righteous living.

A pastor must go beyond simple involvement to a commanding presence. He must take his place at the ship's wheel. The success or failure of the Christian school lies at the pastor's feet. Certainly there is not a "one size fits all" solution to pastoral involvement, but let me suggest the following twenty ideas that may help the pastor enjoy the ride:

1. Establish a written mission and purpose statement for your school
2. Champion excellence through the physical plant and all educational programs.
3. Oversee the school as a church ministry.
4. Have all personnel hold membership in the local church.
5. Insist on a debt-free ministry. Review monthly financial reports.
6. Select a qualified administrator and allow for continuing education.
7. Avoid the day-by-day operation and student discipline.
8. Interview all incoming personnel and make clear the church requirements.
9. Take responsibility for the spiritual tone of the school.
10. Promote the school aggressively in your community.
11. Hold active involvement in your state association and the American Association of Christian Schools.

12. Have a clear policy manual and make it available to all personnel.

13. Treat tuition collection as a business with no exceptions.

14. Update the student handbook periodically and enforce it without preference.

15. Have strict entrance requirements. Test all students for grade placement.

16. Always accept first resignations.

17. Have a parent-orientation and educational program.

18. Set the church and school calendar one year in advance.

19. Take an active roll in chapels and Bible programs.

20. Hold student revivals, Bible camps, and student leadership training.

Juggle the list to fit your situation. There is nothing new, but then again the entire idea of this article is to get all of us pastors back to the basics that made the Christian school movement successful in the first place.

An Arm of the Local Church

Having watched the unfolding of Christian education over these past three decades, I have become more grateful each year to the pastors and churches that support Christian schools. We must never forget that the Christian school movement is an arm of the local church. Make no mistake: our schools will only be as strong as their sponsoring churches. Christian education has faced and will face many dangers, the greatest of which would be the separation of our schools from the hearts of our pastors and from the arms of our local churches.

Conclusion

Pastor, the time is crucial. Christian education should never be content with the status quo. Through solid leadership provided by pastors, we must move forward and take an aggressive posture in training young people. If Christian education was right and if it was Biblical when the movement flourished in the late 60s and 70s, it is still right and Biblical today. Our task now, as it was then, is to equip our generation mentally, physically, socially, and spiritually, enabling excellence in carrying out the will of God in their lives.

Note: We have included this article because of its excellent analysis and its practical call to action. However, not every opinion expressed reflects the viewpoints of the authors of this book.

Appendix 2
For Chapter 2, Reclaiming a School for Christ
Also pertains to Chapters 11-13 on Academics, Music, and Athletics

Awards Descriptions

The following is intended to offer suggestions for awards and recognitions two areas:
1. Honoring excellence of spiritual character as well as honoring success in academics, fine arts, and athletics.
2. Keeping a spiritual emphasis as part of honoring all areas.

This is not intended to be a comprehensive list of awards. Only those pertaining to the above two goals are included.

Character Awards

Student of the Month
Each month a boy and a girl are chosen from each class in grades K through 6 to be student of the month. This award is not an academic award but a character award. It is based upon obedience, hard work, good citizenship, conduct, etc. Each month in kindergarten and elementary chapel, the students chosen are presented a beautiful certificate. Additionally, their names are published in the school newsletter.

School Spirit Award
This year-end award is given to the junior or senior young man and young lady who have shown by their actions and attitudes, and especially by their show of school spirit, that they actively support the school in its direction.

Servant Spirit

This award is given to the junior or senior young man and young lady who have best shown a servant's attitude and a willingness to work in cooperation with the school.

Mr. and Miss [school name]

This award is given to one senior young man and one senior young lady selected by their peers, the members of the junior and senior classes (combined vote for both), as representing the ideals of the school.

Sports Awards

Each spring an athletic awards ceremony is held. At this ceremony outstanding athletes are awarded trophies and plaques recognizing their performance and, more importantly, recognizing their character.

Christian Athlete Award

This is the highest athletic award given, presented to the senior athlete who has best represented Christ on and off the field or court. This is presented at graduation.

Team Player Award

The recipient of this award is the player from each team who best contributes to his or her team in the following areas: Christian character, spiritual leadership, hard work, athletic ability, and team leadership both on and off the field or court. Although no person is perfect, this player best embodies the attributes sought in a Christian athlete.

Most Valuable Player

The recipient of this award is the player who best contributes to his or her team athletically on the field or court.

(This is included for distinction from the Team Player Award.)

Music Awards

Music in Ministry Award

This award is the most prestigious music award offered by the school. It honors both music ability and Christian service in the music ministry of the student's local church. It is given to a senior who demonstrates a heart to glorify God by making biblical choices in the music that he or she listens to or performs, shows a spirit of Christlikeness in attitudes and actions, and participates regularly in the music ministry of a Bible-believing local church of which he or she is a member. In addition to involvement in a church music ministry, the recipient must be a member of at least one music group at the Christian school. This award is presented at graduation.

Music Leadership

This award is given to one boy and one girl who demonstrate musical ability and a desire to glorify God by making biblically sound music choices and who seek to lead others with the attitude of a servant. The recipient must be a member of at least one music group at the Christian school.

Musician Award

This award is given to one boy or girl who, in the opinion of the music faculty and administration, possesses a God-given talent in music in one or more areas. Additionally, the recipient must display a level of artistry beyond his or her peers and a self-disciplined approach to study and performance, while maintaining a spirit of humility. The recipient must be a member of at least one music group at the Christian school.

(As with the Most Valuable Player award in the athletic section, the Musician Award is included to show its difference from the Music Leadership award. There could be variations of this award in each area, such as band and choir.)

Other Commencement awards

Perseverance Award

The purpose of this award is to recognize a senior who has, despite circumstances, sought to bring glory to the Lord with an uncomplaining attitude and a spirit of perseverance, accomplishing tasks beyond what might have been expected. This award is presented to the senior who has exemplified Christian character and determination:

1. To do the best possible job, whatever the circumstances.
2. To persevere when working to accomplish goals.
3. To meet all challenges while leaning upon God's grace with an uncomplaining attitude.
4. To bring glory and honor to the Lord by overcoming difficulties that would defeat some.

Love for the Bible Award

This award takes its name from Psalm 119:47, which says, "And I will delight myself in thy commandments, which I have loved." This award is given to a senior who demonstrates the following characteristics:

1. Achievement in Bible learning.
2. A demonstrated desire for the Word.
3. A realization of its absolute value and place in life.

Complete Person Award

The purpose of this award is to honor the graduating senior who best manifests the qualities spoken of in Colossians 2:6-10: "As ye have therefore received Christ Jesus the Lord, so walk ye in him: Rooted and built up in him, and stablished in the faith, as ye have been taught, abounding therein with thanksgiving. Beware lest any man spoil you through philosophy and vain deceit, after the tradition of men, after the rudiments of the world, and not after Christ. For in him dwelleth all the fulness of the Godhead bodily. And ye are complete in him, which is the head of all principality and power."

The Complete Person Award is presented to a well-rounded graduating senior who has excelled in his or her days at the Christian school in four areas:

1. Spiritual leadership.
2. Athletic excellence.
3. Music excellence.
4. Scholastic achievement.

President's Award

The highest award that is bestowed on a student at the Christian school is the President's Award. This award is presented to a graduating senior who strengthened the spiritual atmosphere of the Christian school through the following:

1. Deep devotion to the Lord Jesus Christ.
2. Outstanding leadership.
3. Consistent character.
4. Desire to excel in every undertaking for God's glory.
5. Dedication to the welfare of fellow students.

Appendix 3

Job Descriptions, Pastor (in relation to school) and Administrator

Every position in the school should have a job description, but that is the subject matter for a book on school management. Only the roles of the pastor and the school administrator are included here. The ability of a Christian school to develop Christlike character is affected by the interaction of these two leaders and their mutual understanding of their roles.

Pastor

The pastor of the church serves as the president of the Christian school. As the head of the school, the pastor provides administrative leadership and spiritual direction. Although the daily operation of the school is delegated to the school's administration, the pastor provides valuable insight and direction in the following areas:

- Input regarding hiring, dismissals, and annual teaching assignments.
- Oversight of the budget process.
- Chapel speaking on a regular basis.
- Speaking at most major school events.
- Guidance in major disciplinary problems that may arise throughout the school year.
- Progress of the school as discussed in regular meetings with the school administrator.

Administrator

The school administrator helps to set the spiritual and academic tone of the school and serves as the major decision-maker for the various daily activities of the school. He meets regularly with the pastor and is responsible for general planning, organizing, and managing of the events of the school in order to insure a quality program which is thoroughly Christian. The administrator's major responsibilities are the following:

- Oversees day-to-day activities.
- Assists in preparing the annual budget.
- Develops and evaluates faculty and staff; hires and dismisses school staff.
- Oversees the alumni program and booster club.
- Develops fundraising activities and the endowment program.
- Oversees curriculum development.
- Oversees the school improvement plan and the accreditation process.
- Oversees marketing, advertising, and public relations.
- Partners with the advisory team in the oversight of discipline, grades, record keeping, and policy development.
- Develops future strategic planning by formulating five-, ten-, fifteen-, and twenty-year plans.

Appendix 4

For chapter 14, School Growth

New Contacts Form

[Name of Christian School]
Prospective Parents/Families

Parent(s) _____

Address _____

_____

Home # _____

Work # _____

Cell # _____

Cell # _____

Email _____

Names and grades of children _____

_____

_____

How did you hear about [Name of Christian School]?

__Ad   __Word of Mouth   __ Telephone book

__Web Site   __ Telephone   Other _____

Date they called: _____ Date we sent packet: _____

Call taken by: _____

Additional Comments:

Contacts Made:

	Date	By whom
Initial contact	_____	_____
Packet sent	_____	_____
Added to contacts	_____	_____
School mailing sent	_____	_____

Appendix 5

Faculty Event Evaluation

While the event is still fresh on your mind, please complete the questions below and submit to the administrator. Comments may be forwarded to another department to assist in future events.

Event:

Date of Event:

What did you like about the event?

What did you dislike about the event?

What are some specific things you would change about the event to make it better?

(Please use other side for additional comments)

Appendix 6
For chapter 14, School Growth

Departure Questionnaire

[Name of Christian School]
Departure Questionnaire

The purpose of this questionnaire is to seek input from parents who have been associated with [name of Christian school]. Please fill out this survey and give us your honest opinions. Thank you for your valuable input and your willingness to help us see where we need to improve. Please complete and return the form this week, while thoughts are still fresh in your mind. A self-addressed, stamped envelope is included for your convenience.

Your child(ren)'s grade(s):
K   1   2   3   4   5   6   7   8   9   10   11   12

Why are you leaving [Name of Christian School]?

How long have you been associated with [Name of Christian School]?

Please use the following scale for questions 4-12:
5 –   Very Pleased
4 –   Pleased
3 –   Indifferent
2 –   Unhappy
1 –   Very unhappy

_____ 4. Communication lines are open between administration, teachers, parents, and students.

_____ 5. Overall satisfaction with the school's communication to the home (telephone calls, newsletters, flyers, letters, etc.).

_____ 6. How do you feel about your student's academic progress at [Name of Christian School]?

_____ 7. How do you rate your student's attitude toward his or her classes at [Name of Christian School]?

_____ 8. How do you rate your attitude toward the administration at [Name of Christian School]?

_____ 9. Which of the numbers in the scale above describes your overall feeling toward [Name of Christian School]?

_____ 10. What curriculum improvement would you like to see at [Name of Christian School]

_____ 11. What building improvement and/or equipment addition would you like to see initiated at [Name of Christian School]?

_____ 12. What, if any, is the school improvement you were most pleased with recently?

Evaluating Departments
Please circle the number that best summarizes the type of education and atmosphere that you feel [Name of Christian School] provides.

Then, on the lines below each set of numbers, state what you believe to be the strengths or weaknesses of each.

SCALE:

5   Superior (far exceeds basic requirements)
4   Excellent (exceeds basic requirements)
3   Average (meets basic requirements)
2   Needs Improvement
1   Unsatisfactory
0   Unable to Answer

BIBLE/CHAPEL   5   4   3   2   1   0
Strengths:
Weaknesses:

ENGLISH   5   4   3   2   1   0
Strengths:
Weaknesses:

MATH   5   4   3   2   1   0
Strengths:
Weaknesses:

SCIENCE   5   4   3   2   1   0
Strengths:
Weaknesses:

HISTORY   5   4   3   2   1   0
Strengths:
Weaknesses:

| VISUAL ARTS | 5 | 4 | 3 | 2 | 1 | 0 |

Strengths:
Weaknesses:

| MUSIC | 5 | 4 | 3 | 2 | 1 | 0 |

Strengths:
Weaknesses:

| ELECTIVES | 5 | 4 | 3 | 2 | 1 | 0 |

Strengths:
Weaknesses:

| SPIRITUAL | 5 | 4 | 3 | 2 | 1 | 0 |

ATMOSPHERE
Strengths:
Weaknesses:

| COMMUNICATION | 5 | 4 | 3 | 2 | 1 | 0 |

Strengths:
Weaknesses:

| DISCIPLINE | 5 | 4 | 3 | 2 | 1 | 0 |

STUCTURE
Strengths:
Weaknesses:

| FACULTY | 5 | 4 | 3 | 2 | 1 | 0 |

Strengths:
Weaknesses:

FACILITIES	5	4	3	2	1	0

Strengths:
Weaknesses:

OVERALL	5	4	3	2	1	0

Strengths:
Weaknesses:

We appreciate the time you took to fill out this questionnaire. Your input is valuable and very much appreciated. Thank you for all of the time you have invested in [Name of Christian School].

We have enjoyed ministering to you and your family.

Our mission is to assist the Christian home in providing a sound education for its children, both academically and spiritually, in a Christ-honoring and caring atmosphere so that each child may be conformed to the image of Christ.

ADDITIONAL COMMENTS/SUGGESTIONS:

Name (optional):